# Fujifilm X-T5 User Reference

A Comprehensive Companion for Mastering the
Features and Functions of the X-T5 Camera

By

Clyde Bertram

# Table of Content

# INTRODUCTION

The Fujifilm X-T5 is not a big change from the X-T4 but more of an upgrade. It replaced the X-T4 and is better in terms of picture quality. It's excellent for photographers who want a small camera with normal controls. The X-T5 has a new tilting touchscreen, a higher resolution at 40.2MP, and impressive video capabilities. Overall, it looks, feels, and works exceptionally well.

The X-T5 camera has a wider ISO range of 64-51,200, a 40.2-megapixel sensor, and can shoot high-quality videos. It records 6.2K/30p and DCI 4K video, with different frame rate options. The electronic shutter can shoot 20 frames per second with continuous autofocus and exposure and 15 frames per second with the mechanical shutter.

This camera has a handy 3-inch tilting screen, two memory card slots, a clear electronic viewfinder, and a stabilization system that helps keep photos sharp even in shaky conditions.

The new camera focuses much faster and can identify eyes and faces better than the X-T5. It has 425 focus points across the entire picture, and its smart technology can recognize animals, birds, vehicles, motorcycles, aircraft, and trains. For super-detailed photos, it can automatically merge 20 frames to create high-quality 160-megapixel images. This is only the second X-Series camera to have a Pixel Shift Multi-Shot.

The XT5 camera has a very quick shutter, can take up to 740 shots on one charge, and has various features like Wi-Fi, Bluetooth, and different shooting modes. The price for the camera body in the UK and US is £1699 / $1799 in Black or Silver.

# CHAPTER 1: GETTING THE CAMERA UP AND RUNNING

## Preparing the Camera for Initial Use

### Shoulder Strap

If you're like me, you might want to skip this part because attaching a camera strap seems easy, right? Well, I've been doing it the wrong way for 30 years. My method made the straps hang awkwardly, and the ends poked my arms. Learn from my mistake and check the diagrams below to properly attach the shoulder strap. (Before you start, look at the camera manual for installing strap clips if they aren't already on.)

1. Put the strap through the small plastic piece and the camera strap hole.

2. Bring the strap back through the plastic piece, then down through the big stopper's hole away from the camera.

3. Pull the strap back up through the nearest hole in the big stopper.

4. Tighten the straps and do the same to attach the other end to the other camera strap hole.

# The Battery

Your camera comes with a rechargeable battery called NP-W235. If you ever need a new battery, get a real Fujifilm one. Using non-genuine batteries might be unsafe and could cause a fire or explosion. Now, let's talk about putting the battery into the camera.

### Inserting the Battery

1. Turn off the camera.

2. Open the battery compartment by sliding the latch towards the camera lens and flipping it open.

3. Insert the battery into the camera with the metal part going in first. Press the battery latch to the side using the battery. If it's hard to put in, check the battery's direction.

4. Close the battery compartment cover and slide the latch back to lock it.

### Removing the Battery

1. Turn off the camera.

2. Open the battery compartment by sliding the latch towards the lens side, then flip it open.

3. Slide the latch away from the battery to remove it.

4. Close the battery compartment cover and slide the latch back to lock it.

### *Battery Charging*

Put the battery in the camera, and use the USB cable and AC adapter to charge it. Connect the plug adapter, plug in the USB cable between the adapter and the camera, and then plug the AC adapter into a wall outlet. Charging takes around 180 minutes. Alternatively, you can use a computer's USB port, which takes about 600 minutes and uses 5V/500mA charging input.

The light on the camera shows the battery status:

- Light on: Battery is charging

- Light off: Battery is fully charged

- Light blinking: Battery error

Consider getting the BC-W235 charger to charge two batteries externally.

## Memory Cards

Memory cards are essential for storing photos and videos in cameras. The Fujifilm X-T5 has two slots for memory cards – one for CFexpress cards in Slot 1 and another for SD cards in Slot 2. You can use a card in each slot, but it's okay if you don't fill both slots.

### *Inserting the Memory Card*

1. Turn off the camera.

2. Open the cover for the memory card slot.

3. Put the memory card in, ensuring the label faces the back of the camera. Push it down until it clicks. The top slot is Slot 1, and the bottom is Slot 2.

4. Close the cover and latch it.

### Removing the Memory Card

1. Turn off the camera and check that the light is not on.

1. Open the cover for the memory card slot.

2. Put the memory card into the camera carefully, then take it out.

3. Close the cover for the memory card slot and secure it.

### Shooting Without a Card

You can take a picture with the camera even without a memory card, but it won't be saved unless there's a memory card. To avoid any issues, consider turning off this option. It's there so that during product demos in stores, people can try out the camera without needing a memory card.

### Configuring Shooting Without a Card

1. Go to the menu, click the settings icon, choose [Button/Dial Setting], and finally select [Shoot Without Card].

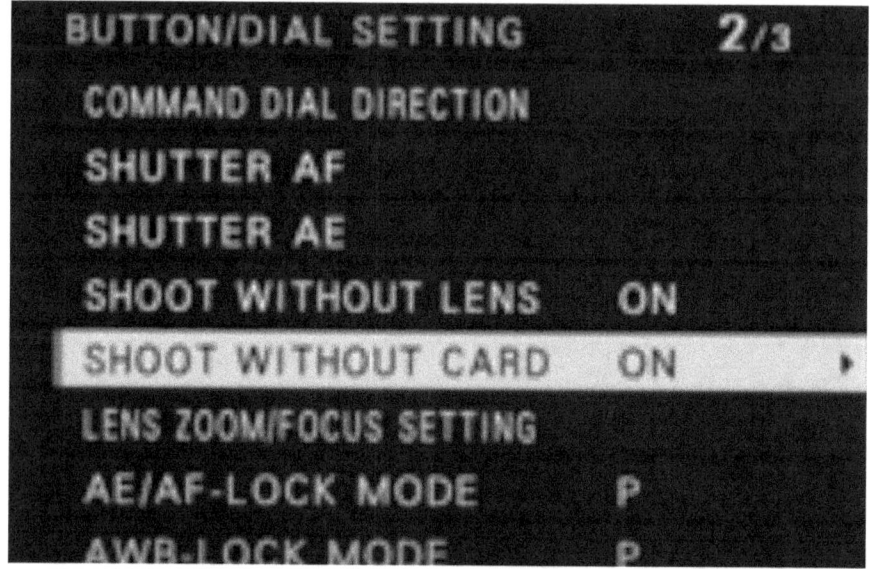

2. Choose:

- **[ON]:** Lets you take a picture even without a memory card.

- **[OFF]:** Prevents the camera from taking a picture without a memory card.

## Lens

### *How to Attach a Lens*

1. Turn left to remove the lens cap from the back of the lens and the cap from the front of the camera.

2. Match the marks on the camera and lens.

3. Slide the lens into the camera and turn it right until it clicks.

### How to Detach a Lens

1. Look at the camera lens, press the lens release button, and turn it counterclockwise until it stops. This is the lens detach button.

2. Take the lens off by pulling it away from the camera. Quickly put the body cap on the camera or switch to another lens. Don't forget to put lens caps on both ends of the removed lens.

### How to Use the Lens

If your camera lens has three adjustable rings—aperture, focus, and zoom—that's great. But not all lenses have an aperture ring; some use the camera to set it. Prime lenses, which don't zoom, obviously skip the zoom ring. There might also be switches on the lens, and we'll talk about those later.

### Shooting Without a Lens Attached

You can take pictures without a lens using the camera. It can be helpful if the Fujifilm X-T5 doesn't recognize your lens. You must set the camera to shoot without a lens in such cases. Additionally, shooting without a lens is necessary if you want to connect your camera to a telescope for astrophotography.

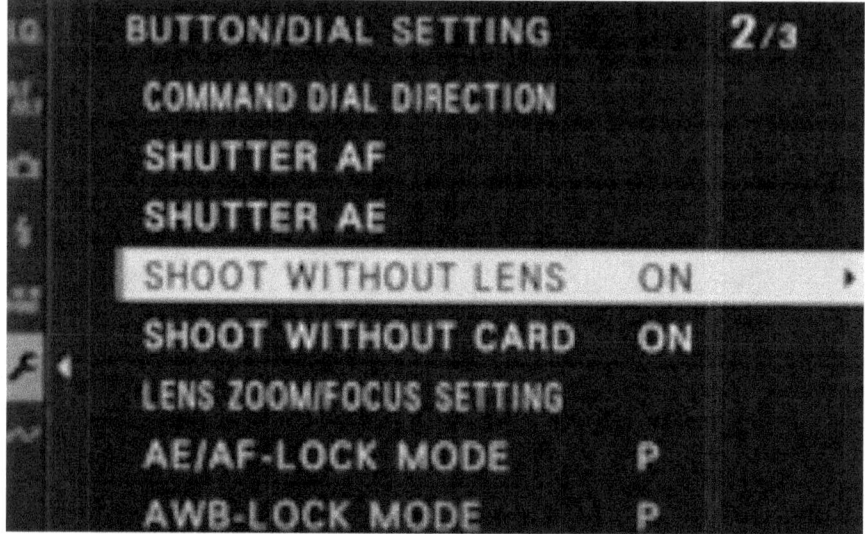

Experiment with "freelensing," also called "lens whacking." This technique involves taking photos without attaching the lens directly to your camera. Instead, hold the lens a bit away from the camera, allowing light to hit the sensor at various angles, creating unique light flare effects in your pictures.

Changing how you hold your camera lens can make your photos look cool. It lets you focus on specific parts of the scene like expensive tilt-shift lenses do. Tilt-shift lenses are easier to focus on compared to freelancing. But be careful; shooting without the lens attached exposes your camera to dust. Consider getting a tilt-shift lens if you want to take many selective focus shots.

You can take close-up pictures of small things by turning the lens around, even if it's not a macro lens. The smaller the mm number on your lens, the closer you get. But it's trickier to focus with wide-angle lenses when free lensing.

# Exploring External Camera Features

## Topside controls

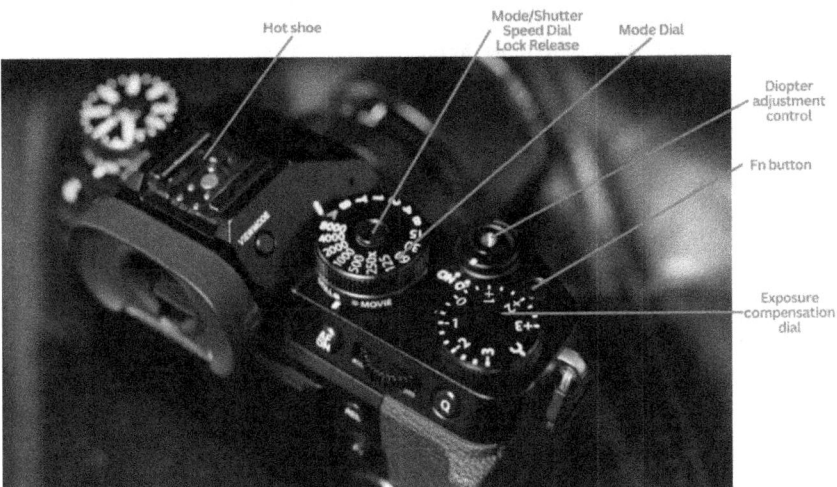

**1. Drive Dial:** The Drive Dial allows you to choose the shooting mode, such as single shot, continuous shooting, or self-timer.

**2. Microphone:** The built-in stereo microphone can be used to record audio during movie recording.

**3. Image Sensor Position Mark:** The Image Sensor Position Mark indicates the position of the image sensor within the camera body. This is helpful for aligning the camera with certain accessories, such as tilt-shift lenses.

**4. <STILL/MOVIE> Mode Dial:** The <STILL/MOVIE> Mode Dial allows you to switch between still photo and movie recording modes.

**5. <ON/OFF> Power Switch:** The <ON/OFF> Power Switch turns the camera on and off.

**6. <Fn1> Button:** The <Fn1> Button can be customized to perform a variety of functions, such as activating the autofocus mode or the white balance setting.

**7. Sensitivity Dial:** The Sensitivity Dial allows you to adjust the ISO speed, which controls the camera's sensitivity to light.

**8. Sensitivity/Drive Mode Dial Lock Release:** The Sensitivity/Drive Mode Dial Lock Release button must be pressed in order to rotate the Sensitivity Dial or Drive Dial.

**9. Diopter Adjustment Control:** The Diopter Adjustment Control allows you to adjust the focus of the viewfinder for your eyesight.

**10. Hot Shoe:** The Hot Shoe allows you to attach external flash units or other accessories.

**11. <VIEW MODE> Button:** The <VIEW MODE> Button allows you to cycle through the different viewfinder displays, such as the optical viewfinder, the electronic viewfinder, and the information display.

**12. <STILL/MOVIE> Mode/Shutter Speed Dial Lock Release:** The <STILL/MOVIE> Mode/Shutter Speed Dial Lock Release button must be pressed in order to rotate the <STILL/MOVIE> Mode Dial or the Shutter Speed Dial.

**13. Shutter Speed Dial:** The Shutter Speed Dial allows you to adjust the shutter speed, which controls the length of time that the camera's shutter remains open for each shot.

**14. Shutter Button:** The Shutter Button takes a picture when pressed.

**15. Exposure Compensation Dial:** The Exposure Compensation Dial allows you to adjust the exposure level of your photos and videos.

## Front features

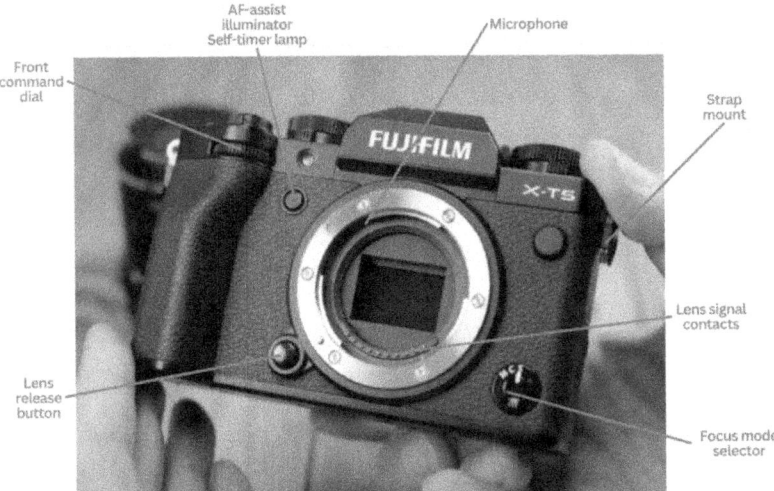

**1. Front Command Dial:** This customizable dial lets you adjust settings like aperture, exposure, or film simulation by rotating it left or right. You can personalize its function in the camera's menus.

**2. <Fn2> Button:** Similar to the Fn1 button on the top, you can assign a specific function to this button for quick access, such as activating focus peaking or bracketing.

**3. Sensor:** This is the heart of the camera, capturing light and transforming it into the beautiful images you see. The X-T5 boasts a powerful APS-C X-Trans CMOS 5 HR sensor with 40.2 megapixels for stunning detail and dynamic range.

**4. Lens Release Button:** Pressing this button disengages the lens from the camera body, allowing you to swap lenses quickly and easily.

**5. AF-Assist Illuminator / Self Timer Lamp/ Tally Light:** This small light assists the autofocus system in low-light conditions. It also doubles as a self-timer lamp and tally light, signaling when recording video.

**6. Sync Terminal:** This port allows you to connect the camera to external studio flash units using a flash synchronization cable.

**7. Lens fitting mark:** This red dot aligns with the corresponding mark on your lens for proper mounting.

**8. Lens Signal Contacts:** These electronic contacts transmit data between the camera and the lens, enabling features like autofocus and aperture control.

**9. Focus Mode Selector:** This lever lets you switch between different autofocus modes, like single autofocus (AF-S), continuous autofocus (AF-C), and manual focus (MF).

**10. Camera Strap Eyelet:** Attach your camera strap here for secure carrying and to prevent accidental drops.

**11. 3.5mm Microphone Jack:** Plug in an external microphone for high-quality audio recording during video shooting.

**12. 2.5mm Remote Release Connector:** Use a remote release cable connected here to trigger the shutter remotely, minimizing camera shake and ideal for long exposures.

**13. Type C USB Connector:** This port serves multiple functions: charging the camera battery, transferring photos and videos to your computer, and updating the camera's firmware.

**14. Speaker:** This built-in speaker lets you playback recorded audio directly from the camera.

**15. Type D HDMI Micro connector:** Connect the camera to an external monitor or projector through this port for high-resolution video output.

**16. Camera Strap Eyelet:** Another strap attachment point for added security and convenience.

**17. Memory Card Slot 2:** Expand your storage capacity by inserting a second SD card here.

**18. Memory Card Slot 1:** Insert your primary SD card into this slot for capturing photos and videos.

# Back-of-the-body controls

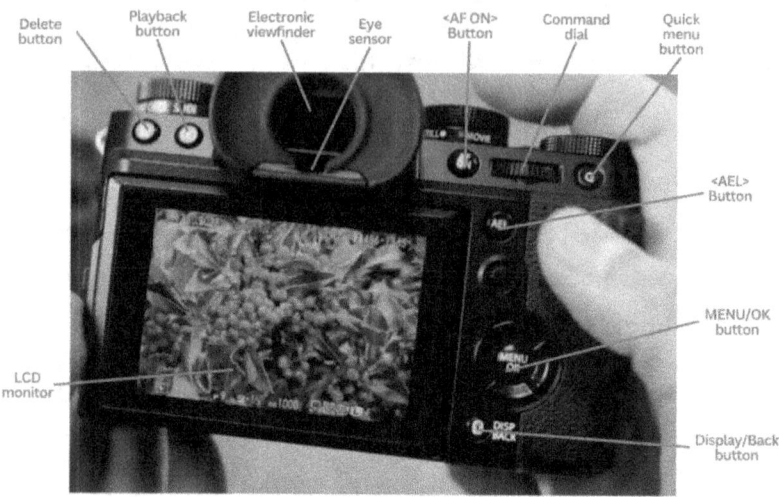

**1. <Delete> Button:** This button permanently removes unwanted photos or videos from the memory card. Use it with caution!

**2. <Playback> Button:** Press this button to enter playback mode, where you can review captured photos and videos.

**3. Eye Cup:** This rubber cushion surrounds the electronic viewfinder (EVF) and helps block out stray light for a more comfortable viewing experience.

**4. Electronic Viewfinder (EVF):** This high-resolution display shows a real-time view of the scene you're framing, allowing you to compose your shots and adjust settings accurately.

**5. <AF ON> Button:** Press this button to activate autofocus, locking the focus on your chosen subject.

**6. <AEL> Button:** This button locks the exposure level, preventing it from changing even if you recompose the shot.

**7. Rear Command Dial:** Similar to the front command dial, you can customize this dial to quickly adjust settings like aperture, shutter speed, or ISO.

**8. <Q> Quick Menu Button:** Press this button to access a context-sensitive menu with frequently used settings for quick adjustments.

**9. Indicator/Tally Lamp:** This small light serves two purposes: indicating camera status (e.g., autofocus lock) and acting as a tally light while recording video.

**10. Focus Stick:** This lever allows you to manually move the focus point within the frame for precise focus control.

**11. <▲> Selector Button:** Navigate menus and settings by pressing this button to move upwards.

**12. <MENU/OK> Button:** Opens the main menu for accessing all camera settings and functions. Also confirms selections within menus.

**13. LCD Monitor/ Touch Screen:** The fully articulating touchscreen LCD allows you to review captured images and videos, compose shots in live view, and navigate menus through touch.

**14. Eye Sensor:** This sensor automatically switches between the EVF and LCD monitor based on whether you bring your eye to the viewfinder.

**15. <DISP/BACK> Display/Back/Bluetooth Button:** Controls various functions depending on the context: in shooting mode, it changes the LCD display information; in playback mode, it returns to the previous image; and it also activates Bluetooth pairing with your smartphone.

**16. <◄> Selector Button:** Navigate menus and settings by pressing this button to move left.

**17. <▼> Selector Button:** Navigate menus and settings by pressing this button to move downwards.

**18. <►> Selector Button:** Navigate menus and settings by pressing this button to move right.

# CHAPTER 2: FOCUSING

## Focus Modes

You need to answer two questions when deciding which focusing mode to pick.

### 1. Who will do the focusing?

Do you want the camera to focus on its own? Choose either Single Autofocus or Continuous Autofocus.

Or do you want to focus manually for full control? Pick Manual Focus mode.

### 2. When will focus occur?

Should the camera focus and stay focused when you press the shutter button halfway (Single AF [AF-S]), or should it keep focusing continuously while the button is pressed (Continuous AF [AF-C])? Now, let's explore the three focus modes you can choose from: [S], [C], and [M].

### Single Auto Focus

Use Single AF (AF-S) when your subject isn't moving, like for landscape or posed portrait shots. With [AF-S], the camera focuses automatically when you press the shutter button halfway, and the focus stays fixed while the button is held halfway.

### Continuous Auto Focus

Continuous AF, or AF-C, is great for capturing things on the go, like moving cars or sports. When you hold the shutter button halfway, the camera adjusts the focus to track the subject's movement. When you take the picture, it tries to guess where the subject will be. For instance, if someone walks towards you, you press the button halfway to focus when they're 20 feet away.

Press the shutter button fully when the person is 10 feet away. If you use AF-S, your subject might be out of focus because the camera only focused once when you pressed the shutter halfway, and the person was 20 feet away. But with AF-C, the camera keeps focusing as the person moves, so they're more likely to stay in focus when they get closer.

**Manual Focus**

Finally, there's manual focus. In this mode, the camera won't help you focus – it's your job to adjust it. Use manual focus for videos or when the autofocus isn't working well. Just turn the focus ring on the lens to manually focus.

# Auto Focus Mode

If you picked [AF-S] or [AF-C] for the Focus Mode, you must choose where the camera focuses. Adjust the autofocus area if the camera focuses on the wrong thing. The camera looks for contrasting areas to focus on using different focus points.

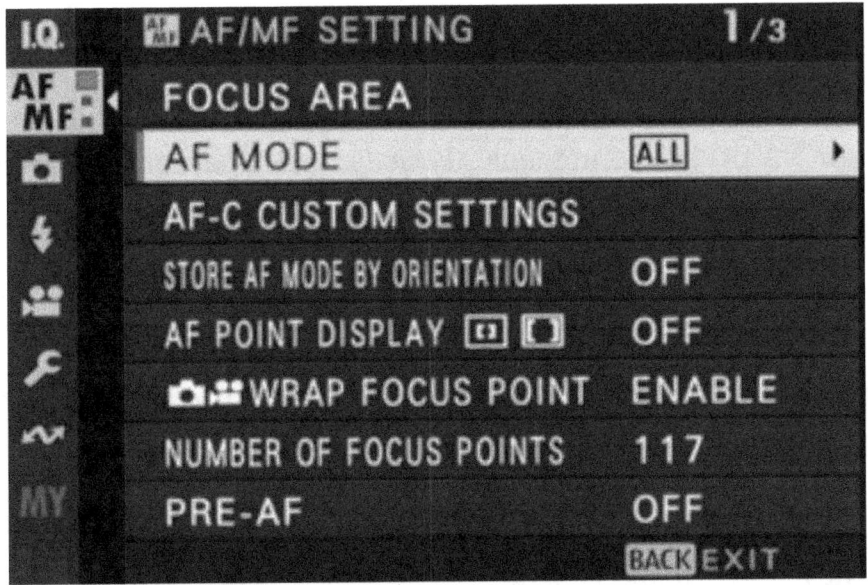

Now, let's check out the auto-focus options.

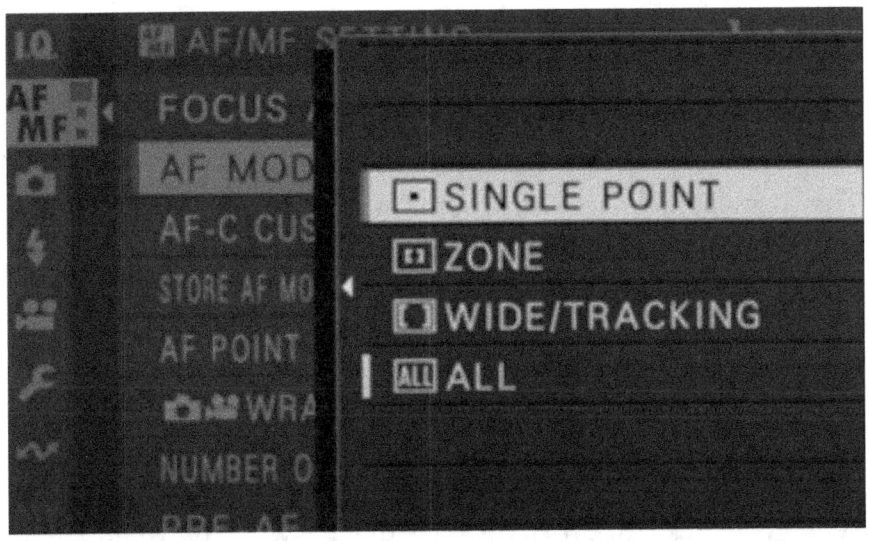

**Single Point**

Single point lets you pick where the camera focuses on the screen, which is helpful for small subjects. Use the focus stick to move the focus spot and the rear command dial to adjust its size. In [AF-C] Continuous AF mode, the camera follows and focuses on the selected point, which is ideal for moving subjects.

## Zone

The camera divides the picture into different focus sections. Each section has several focus points arranged in a grid (7x7, 5x5, or 3x3) to help focus on moving objects. Adjust the focus zone by tilting the focus stick and changing its size by turning the rear command dial.

When you choose [AF-C] Continuous AF mode, the camera will follow and focus on the subject within the chosen focus zone. It works well for subjects moving predictably.

## Wide/Tracking

The camera focuses on parts of the picture with strong contrasts. It uses all the focus points to find those areas. You'll see green frames showing where it's focusing. If you set the focus mode to [AF-C] Continuous AF, the camera will keep tracking a moving subject.

## All

When you pick [All], turn the back dial to switch between Single Point, Zone, and Wide/Tracking focus modes on the display.

## Selecting an Auto Focus Mode

<Choose "AF/MF" from the Menu, then select "AF MODE."

# Auto Focusing in Movie Mode

To take pictures, start by choosing a focus mode: <S> for Single AF, <C> for Continuous AF, or <M> for Manual focus using the focus mode selector. If you go with <S> or <C>, decide where you want the camera to focus.

## How to Select the Focus Point for Video Recording

1.  Go to the Menu and navigate to the AF MODE.

2.  Choose from these options:

    - **MULTI:** The camera picks focus points automatically.

    - **AREA:** The camera focuses where you set the focus area.

    If you pick AREA, you must specify the focus area in the next section.

## Focus Area

After picking an [AF MODE], you can choose where the camera focuses by turning on the focus point display. It shows a grid of tiny squares, and a green frame shows where the camera will look for subjects. You can adjust the focus frame's position and size using the focus stick and rear command dial.

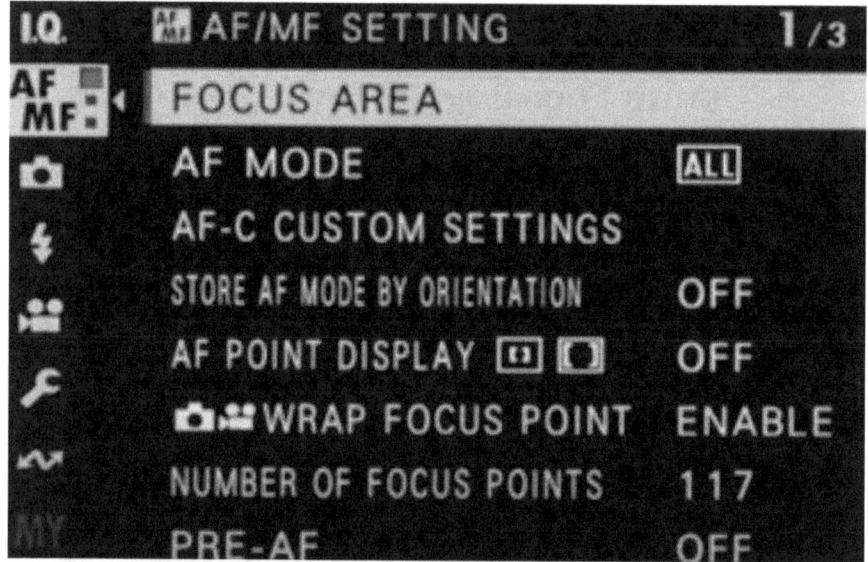

**Enabling the Focus-Point Display for Still Images**

Click on Menu, select AF/MF, then choose Focus Area.

**Enabling the Focus-Point Display for Movie Recording**

Select [AF/MF] in the Menu, then choose [FOCUS AREA].

1. Move the focus frame by tilting the focus stick.

2. Press the focus stick to bring the focus frame back to the center.

3. If the AF Mode is set to Single Point or Zone:

    • Adjust the size of the focus frame by turning the rear command dial left or right.

    • Press the rear command dial to reset the focus frame to its default size.

# AF Point Display

If you set <MENU>→ [AF/MF] → [AF MODE] to [Wide]/[Tracking] or [Zone], you can decide if you want to see the focus frames used for focusing.

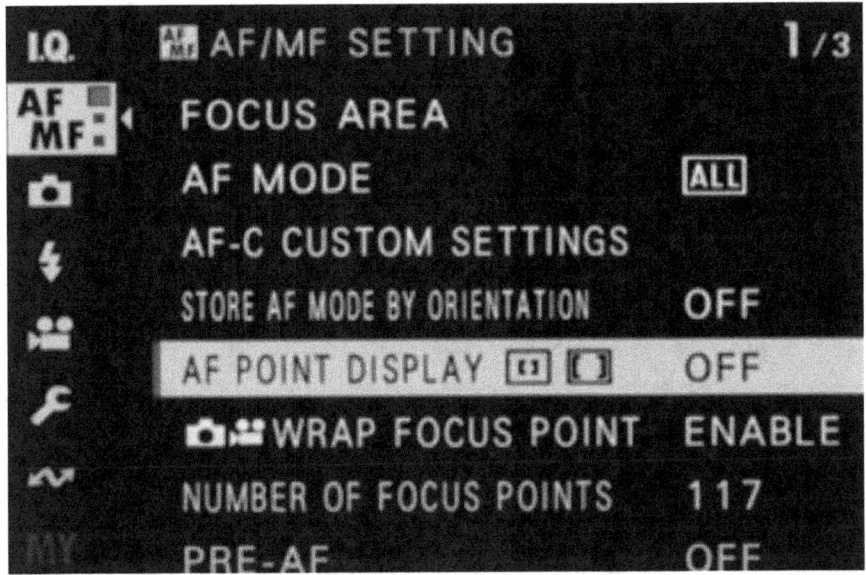

To turn on/off the focus point display:

1. <MENU>→ [AF/MF] → [AF POINT DISPLAY]

2. Choose:

   - **[ON]:** Show focus points.

   - **[OFF]:** Hide focus points.

# Number of Focus Points

When you're manually focusing or using the single-point autofocus mode on your camera, you have the power to decide how many focus points you want to use. It's like picking how many tiny spots on the screen you want the camera to pay attention to when trying to get your shot just right. This choice lets you be in control of where the camera focuses, making it easier for you to capture the perfect image.

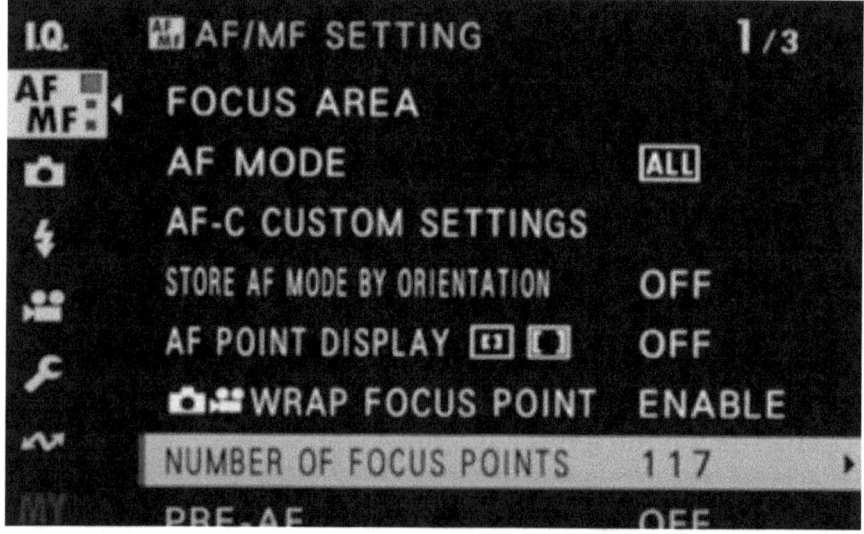

To set the number of focus points:

1. Go to the Menu and select [AF/MF].

2. Choose [NUMBER OF FOCUS POINTS]:

    - **[117 POINTS (9X13)]:** Pick from 117 focus points in a 9 x 13 grid.

- **[425 POINTS (17 x 25)]:** Choose from 425 focus points in a 17 x 25 grid.

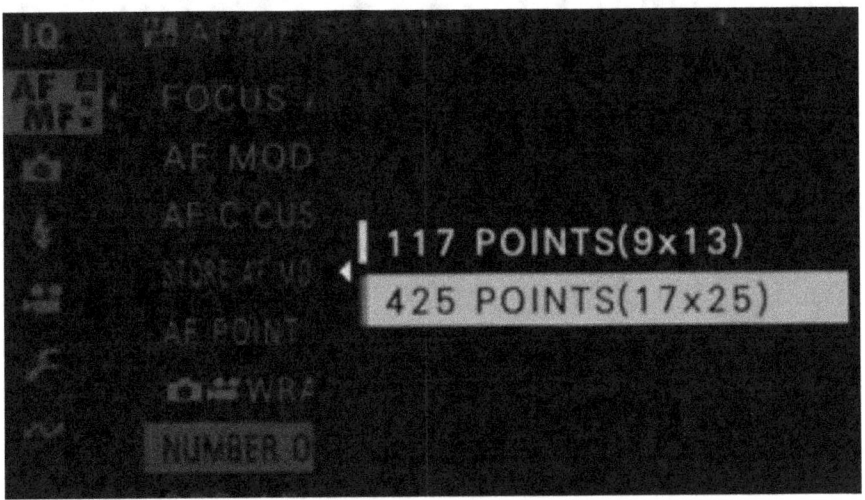

## Wrap Focus Point

To simplify moving the focus frame on your camera, you can decide what happens when it reaches the edge of the screen. You have two options: it can either stay where it is or jump to the opposite side.

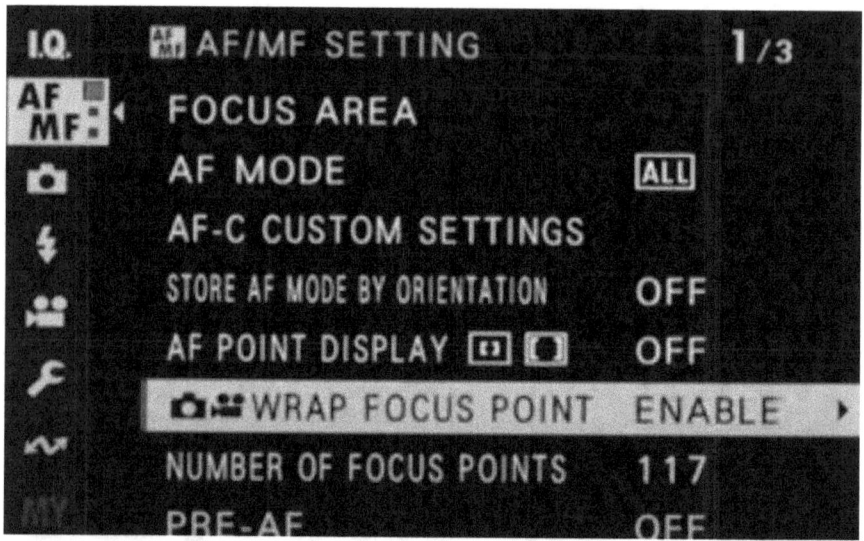

For example, if the focus frame is on the far right and you try to move it further right off the screen, it will either stay on the right side or quickly jump to the far left side. This way, you can choose the behavior that works best for you when adjusting the focus frame.

**Setting Wrap Focus Point**

1. Go to the Menu, choose AF/MF, then select Wrap Focus Point.

2. Choose:

   • **Enable:** If moved beyond the screen edge, the focus frame jumps to the opposite end.

   • **Disable:** The focus frame won't go past the screen edge.

# Pre-AF

Set the camera to focus ahead of time for quicker operation. If you keep the camera still, it can focus while you wait to capture the perfect moment. When you press the shutter button, focusing will be faster than if the camera didn't focus in advance.

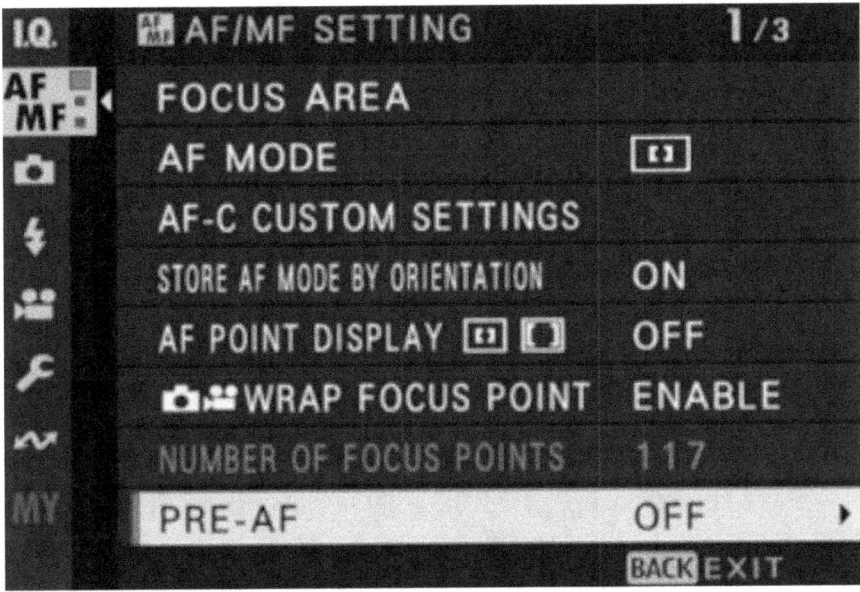

Remember, focusing ahead of time will use up the battery faster. With [PRE-AF] turned [ON], the camera will constantly adjust focus in [AF-S] and [AF-C] modes, even without pressing the shutter button.

**Enabling/Disabling Pre-AF**

Choose between auto-focus (AF) and manual focus (MF), then select pre-auto-focus (PRE-AF) and decide whether to turn it on or off.

# Release/Focus Priority

When you pick either AF-S or AF-C focus mode on your camera, you get to decide whether the camera should first focus and then take a picture, or just go ahead and capture the shot without waiting to focus. It's like choosing whether you want the camera to make sure everything's clear before snapping the photo, or if you're okay with it taking the shot quickly, focusing as it goes.

**Configuring Release/Focus Priority**

1. Go to the Menu, choose AF (Auto Focus) and MF (Manual Focus), and pick either RELEASE or FOCUS PRIORITY.

2. If you choose RELEASE, the camera immediately takes a picture when you press the shutter, even if the subject is not focused. If you choose FOCUS, the camera waits to take a picture until it focuses on the subject.

# Store AF Mode By Orientation

If you often switch between taking pictures in vertical and horizontal positions, turning on the [STORE AF MODE BY ORIENTATION] setting helps the camera remember your focus settings. For example, if it's set to [ON], you can use Single Point AF Mode with the focus point in the upper right when you shoot horizontally. When you switch to shooting vertically, the camera remembers to use Zone AF Mode with the focus point still in the upper right.

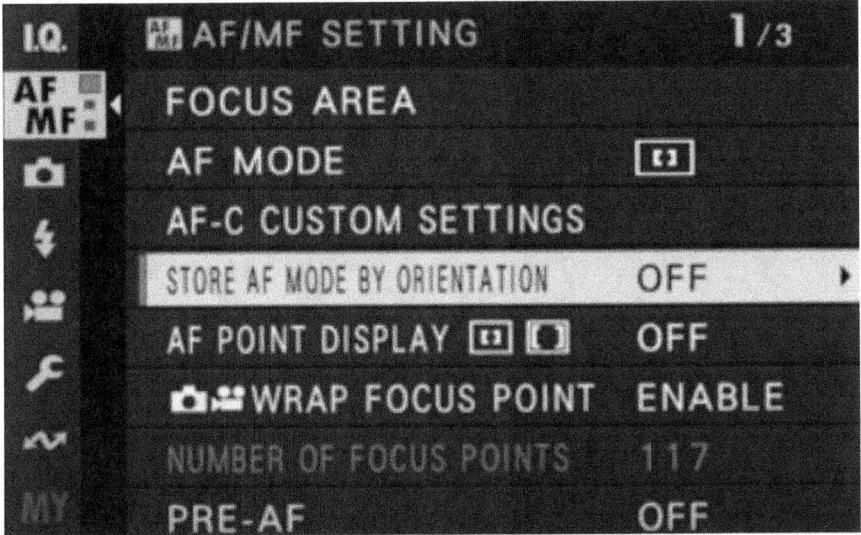

Now, when I turn the camera, it remembers where and how I focused in each position. If I turn the camera sideways, the focus point goes to the upper right in landscape, and if I turn it vertically in portrait, the focus point moves to the lower right. But if I chose only to store the focus area in the landscape, the focus point would be in the upper right. When turned to portrait, the focus point moves to the lower right, but the focus mode stays as Single Point AF instead of switching to Zone AF.

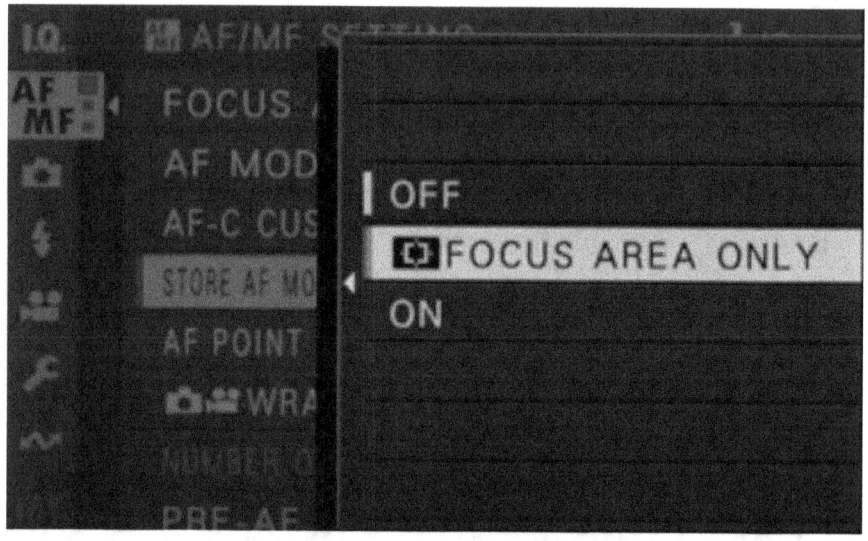

## Setting Store AF Mode by Orientation

1.  Go to the Menu, choose Auto Focus (AF) and Manual Focus (MF), then select to store the AF mode based on the camera's orientation.

2.  Choose one of the following:

    -   **OFF:** Focus settings stay the same regardless of the camera's orientation.

    -   **FOCUS AREA ONLY:** Focus area position adjusts with camera orientation, but focus mode stays constant.

    -   **ON:** Both focus mode and focus frame position change based on the camera's orientation.

# AF Range Limiter

When you're using autofocus on your camera, you have the option to decide how much of the scene the camera should consider when trying to focus. If you make this range smaller, the autofocus works faster because the camera only needs to look for focus within a certain distance instead of scanning the entire scene. It's like telling the camera to focus on something nearby or far away, depending on your preference.

### Configuring the Auto Focus Limits

1. Go to the camera menu, choose autofocus (AF) or manual focus (MF), and select autofocus range limiter.

2. You can turn it off, set custom minimum and maximum focus distances, use pre-defined presets, or confirm your custom settings by navigating the Menu using the selector buttons. Adjust the focus distances and press the appropriate buttons to save your changes.

# Back Button Focus

If you choose an autofocus, you can decide how the camera focuses. Usually, when you press the shutter button halfway, the camera focuses; when you press it fully, it takes a picture. This is the default. But there's another way: some photographers use a separate <AF ON> button for focusing, called back button focus. So, instead of the shutter button, you'd use the <AF ON> button to autofocus.

Back button focus lets you easily switch between automatic and manual focus. Press the <AF ON> button to autofocus; don't press it to keep your focus without the camera autofocusing.

Using back button focus means the camera focuses when you press a specific button, not when you take the picture. It helps you capture photos faster by skipping the focusing step when pressing the shutter button. Also, it reduces the chance of missing a shot because autofocus might not get it right on the first try. To use back button focus, set [SHUTTER AF] to [OFF] for both [AF-S] and [AF-C].

## Setting Shutter AF

★ Go to the Menu, navigate to the AF/MF section, find the BUTTON/DIAL SETTING, and choose SHUTTER AF.

★ Choose how you want the shutter button to work:

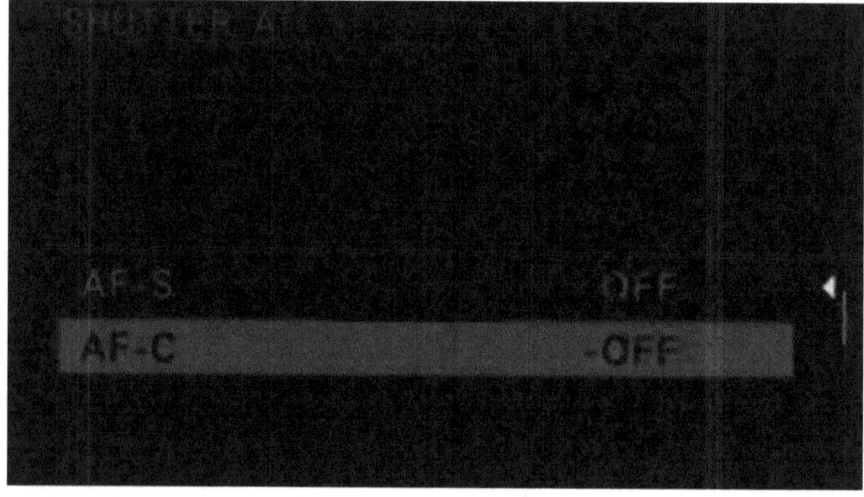

- For [AF-S] mode:

  - **[ON]:** Focus locks when you press the button halfway.

  - **[OFF]:** No autofocus when you press the button halfway.

- For [AF-C] mode:

  - **[ON]:** The camera keeps focusing as long as you press the button halfway.

  - **[OFF]:** No autofocus when you press the button halfway.

## How to Take a Picture with Back Button Focus

1. Use the <AF-ON> button to make the camera focus automatically on your subject.

2. Push the shutter button to capture a picture.

# Manual Focus

Manual focusing is when the person using the camera is in charge of adjusting the focus, which is how sharp or clear the image appears. This is useful for shooting videos because when the camera focuses on its own, it might cause the footage to be shaky. With manual focus, the person can smoothly change the focus from one thing to another, making the video look more polished and professional.

## Using Manual Focus

1.  Move the focus mode selector to <M>.

2.  Turn the focus ring on the lens to focus manually. Rotate left to get closer focus and right to focus farther. You can switch this if you want.

## Setting the Focus Ring Direction

1.  Go to the Menu by tapping the settings icon, choose button/dial settings, then lens zoom/focus settings, and finally select focus ring rotate.

2.  Choose CW to increase focus distance by rotating the focus ring clockwise or CCW to increase focus distance by rotating it counterclockwise. The X-T5 also lets you pick how focus changes when you move the focus ring.

## Setting the Focus Ring Operation

1.  Go to the settings menu, then navigate to button/dial settings, lens zoom/focus settings, and finally, focus ring operation.

2.  Choose between two options:

    *   **Nonlinear:** Focus changes as much as you turn the focus ring.

    *   **Linear:** Focus changes based on how much you turn the ring but is not influenced by the speed of your rotation.

If you have enabled the manual focus distance indicator in the screen set up under the Menu and settings, a graph will show on the screen as you adjust the focus ring.

The manual focus indicator tells you how close or far your camera is focused on the subject. The white line shows the distance to the subject, and the blue bar indicates the range in front of and behind the subject that will be in focus. If you're using autofocus, a similar indicator called AF DISTANCE INDICATOR is available in the settings menu.

## Setting the Focus Indicator Scale Units

Go to the Menu, click the setting icon, choose screen set-up, then pick either meters or feet for focus scale units. You can also customize the depth of field part of the distance indicators.

## Setting the Depth-of-Field Scale

1. Go to the Menu, choose between auto-focus (AF) and manual focus (MF), then select the depth-of-field scale.

2. Pick either a pixel basis for images on screens or a film format basis for images that will be printed to decide the depth of field.

# Focus Zoom

If you're taking photos or videos and struggling to see where your camera is focused, use the Focus Zoom feature. In focus mode <S>, press the center of the rear dial to zoom in. Move

41

the enlarged area by tilting the focus stick and adjust the zoom by turning the rear dial <>. To exit the zoomed view, press the center of the rear dial again.

## Focus Check

If you're using Manual focus, turn on Focus Check. When Focus Check is ON, the camera zooms in on the focus area automatically when you turn the focus ring. It makes it easier to see small details because the view is magnified.

### Enabling/Disabling Focus Check for Still images

<Choose [AF/MF] from the Menu, then go to [FOCUS CHECK], and finally, pick either [ON] or [OFF].

### Enabling/Disabling Focus Check for Video Recording

Choose between auto-focus (AF) and manual focus (MF), then go to the focus check option and decide whether to turn it on or off.

Turn the back dial to zoom in or out. Press the center of the same dial to go back from the zoomed-in view.

## Focus Check Lock

If you turn on Focus Check, you can decide if you want the screen to stay zoomed in when recording a video. If you set Focus Check Lock to [ON], the screen stays zoomed in, but the actual video won't be zoomed in when you watch it later.

## Enabling/Disabling Focus Check for Video Recording

Choose between autofocus (AF) and manual focus (MF), then go to the "FOCUS CHECK LOCK" option and select either "ON" or "OFF."

# Chapter 3: Choosing Basic Picture Settings

## Drive Settings

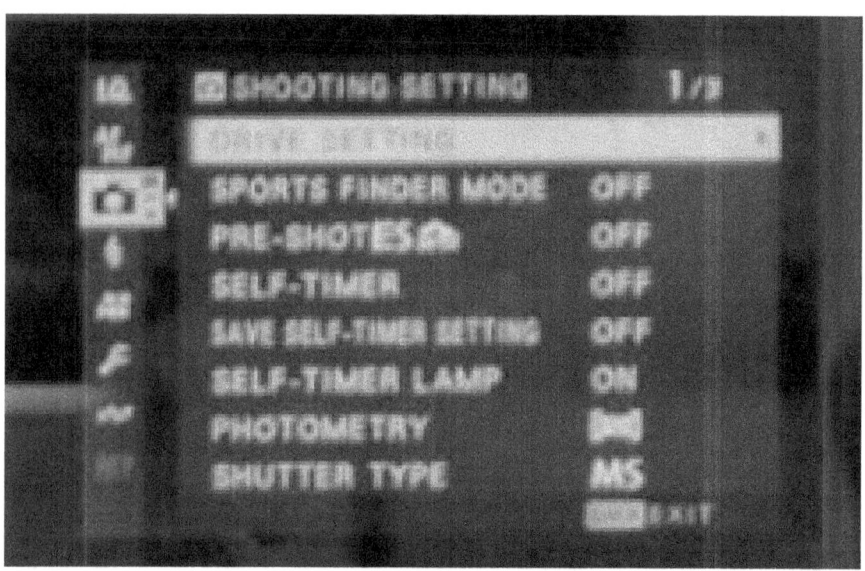

### Drive Modes

The drive mode is like a camera setting that decides what happens when you press the button to take a picture. Just turn the drive dial to pick the setting you want.

### Selecting a Drive Mode

1. Turn the dial to choose a mode:

   - **Panorama:** Capture a wide image.

- **[ADV]:** Use advanced filter effects.

- **[BKT] Bracket:** Pick settings like exposure, ISO, and more for a series of shots.

- **[CH] CONTINUOUS HIGH SPEED BURST:** Take several quick shots while holding the shutter button. Faster than CONTINUOUS LOW SPEED BURST.

- **[CL] CONTINUOUS LOW-SPEED BURST:** Take consecutive shots at a slower pace by holding the shutter button.

- **[S] Single frame:** Snap one picture with each shutter button press.

- **[HDR]:** Capture an image with high dynamic range.

## Continuous Shooting Drive Modes

When you use continuous shooting mode, the camera takes many pictures, one after the other, while holding the button. It stops when you let go. It is handy for capturing fast-moving scenes or when you're unsure when the best moment will happen. It's also helpful in creating a sequence of still images showing motion.

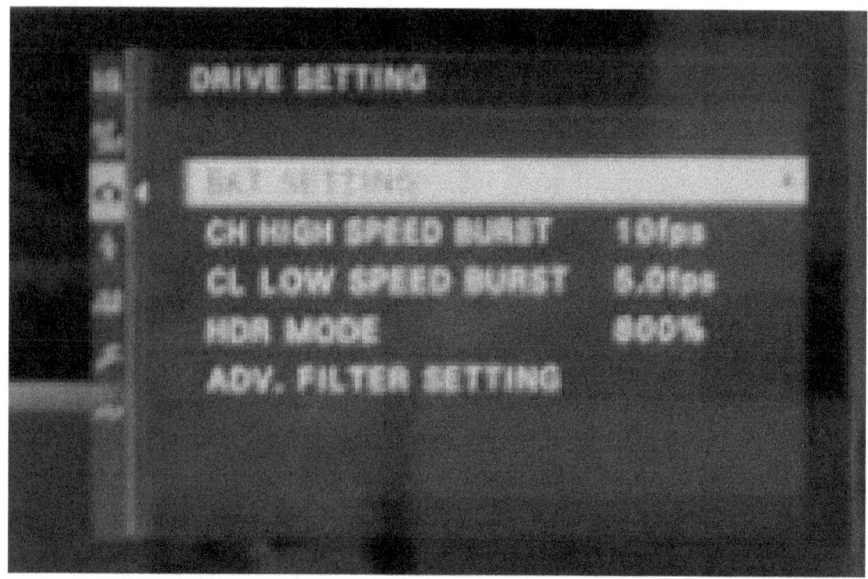

The X-T5 camera gives you two choices for taking multiple pictures in a row: CH (high-speed burst) and CL (low-speed burst). CH is faster, taking pictures quickly in a sequence, while CL is slower. If you want to see your subjects in real time while taking pictures, choose CL for a better view.

When you take many pictures in a row quickly, the speed might decrease. The default setting keeps the brightness the same in all those pictures. If you want each picture to have a different brightness, go to the Menu, find "Setting," then "BUTTON/DIAL SETTING," and turn off "SHUTTER AE."

### Configuring Continuous Shooting

1. Turn the dial to CH or CL.

2. Go to MENU, then [Camera icon], and choose [DRIVE SETTING] to set the frame rate.

46

3.  For high-speed burst, pick from these options:

    *   20 frames per second (1.29x crop) with electronic shutter.

    *   13 frames per second (1.29x crop) with electronic shutter.

    *   15 frames per second with mechanical shutter or 13 fps with electronic shutter.

4.  10 frames per second with mechanical shutter or 8.9 fps with electronic shutter.

    *   For low-speed burst (CL), choose from:

    *   7 frames per second with mechanical shutter or 6.7 fps with electronic shutter.

    *   5 frames per second.

    *   3 frames per second.

## Shutter Type

The Fuji X-T5 gives you options for how the camera takes pictures. You can pick a mechanical shutter, like what DSLRs use, with physical curtains opening and closing each shot. Alternatively, you can let the camera decide based on the shooting conditions.

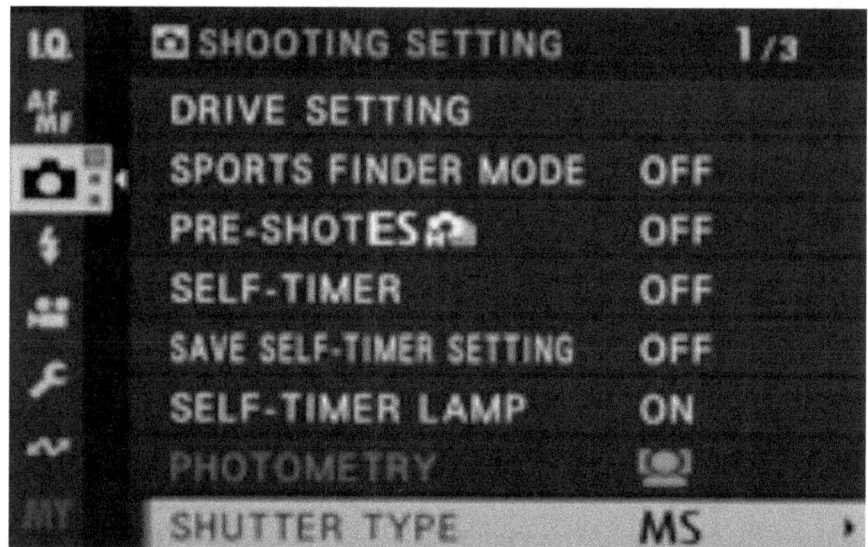

An electronic shutter simply switches the camera sensor on and off to take a picture without moving parts. It's quiet, reduces camera shake, and can capture images faster than a traditional shutter.

When using an electronic shutter, the pictures might get messed up, especially when capturing fast movement or changing light, like with a flash. This happens because the sensor exposes different parts of the image at different times. Imagine a garage door going up and down – the sensor starts at the top, becomes sensitive to light, reads one line at a time, and moves down until the whole picture is taken.

Usually, this happens fast, and we don't usually see it. However, problems arise when you move the camera or capture very fast-moving things, like an airplane propeller. Fast camera movements can make the picture shake like jello (that's why it's called the jello effect), and straight lines can get distorted.

If you take pictures indoors using a camera's electronic shutter, the lighting can create a weird pattern in your photos. This happens because indoor lights flicker quickly, and the camera might capture some parts of the photo as bright and others as dark, making a striped effect. This is also why using a flash with an electronic shutter can be tricky – the flash is so quick that only specific areas of the photo might get lit up.

To capture fast-moving things, use the regular shutter on the Fuji X-T5. There's also a mode called E-Front Curtain Shutter, which uses an electronic start to prevent shaking and then switches to the normal shutter to avoid certain issues. However, this mode isn't completely silent and is not ideal for very fast shutter speeds or when using a flash.

### *Selecting a Shutter Type*

1. Go to the camera settings by tapping on the Menu, then choose the shutter type by selecting the camera icon.

2. Choose one of the following shutter options:

    - **Mechanical Shutter (MS):** Only uses the mechanical shutter.

    - **Electronic Shutter (ES):** Only uses the electronic shutter. Can select shutter speeds faster than 1/8000 sec by adjusting the dials.

49

- **E-Front Curtain Shutter (EF):** Uses a hybrid of electronic shutter to start exposure and mechanical shutter to end exposure.

- **Mechanical + Electronic (M+E):** Automatically switches between mechanical and electronic shutter based on conditions. Can select shutter speeds faster than 1/8000 sec.

- **E-Front + Mechanical (EF+M):** Automatically switches between E-Front curtain shutter and mechanical shutter based on conditions.

- **E-Front + Mechanical + Electronic (EF+M+E):** Automatically selects between mechanical, electronic, or E-Front curtain shutter based on conditions. Can select shutter speeds faster than 1/8000 sec by adjusting the dials.

## Pre-Shot ES

To reduce the delay between pressing the camera button and taking a picture, use [PRE-SHOT ES] by setting the drive dial to [CH] and choosing [ES ELECTRONIC SHUTTER] in the Menu under [Camera icon] → [SHUTTER TYPE]. With [PRE-SHOT ES], the camera captures images as soon as you press the shutter button halfway, allowing your burst photos to start slightly before fully pressing the button.

### Enabling/Disabling Pre-Shot ES

Choose whether to turn the "PRE-SHOT ES" feature on or off by navigating through the Menu using the camera icon.

## Bracket Setting

Bracket Setting on the X-T5 camera is like taking a bunch of pictures with different setups. It's like having six different superheroes with special powers! The camera can automatically create sets of pictures with varying settings in six cool ways:

- **ISO Bracketing:** It takes shots at different ISO levels, giving you pictures with varying brightness.

- **White Balance Bracketing:** This one captures images with different color balances, like having photos with warmer or cooler tones.

- **Exposure Bracketing:** It takes pictures with different exposure levels, so you get some bright ones, some dark ones, and one in the middle.

- **Film Simulation Bracketing:** This is like changing the film in an old-school camera. It creates pictures with different styles, making your photos look unique.

- **Dynamic Range Bracketing:** Imagine it as capturing pictures with different levels of contrast, making some parts stand out more.

- **Focus Bracketing:** This is like taking pictures where different things are in focus. It's handy for those times when you want to highlight different parts of a scene.

## *ISO BKT*

When you use ISO bracketing while taking a photo, your camera does something pretty neat. Instead of just one picture, it grabs three! The first picture is taken with the ISO setting you picked. Then, it snaps another with a lower ISO and a third with a higher ISO. Imagine your ISO is set at 400, and you choose a bracketing range of [+-1]. Now, you end up with three images: one at ISO 400, another at ISO 200 (lowered by 1 stop), and the third at ISO 800 (raised by 1 stop).

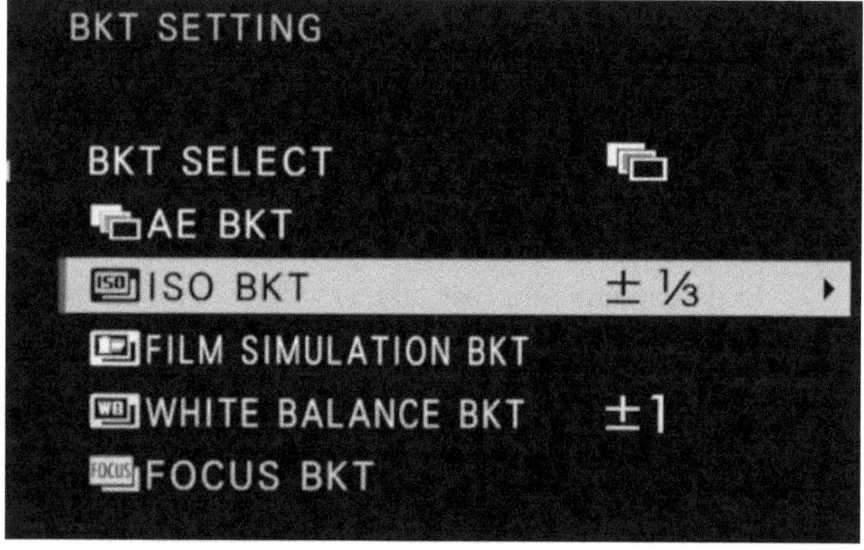

Using ISO Bracketing

1. Turn the dial to <BKT>.

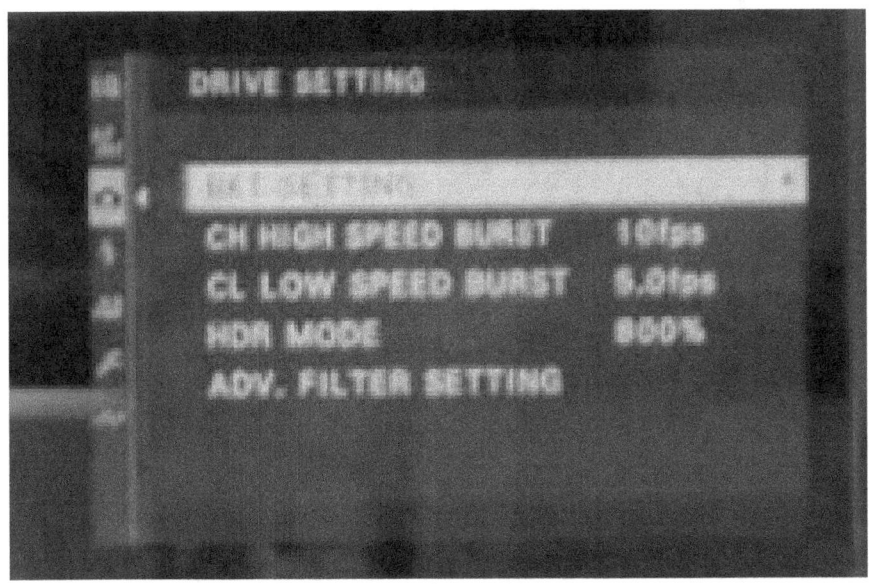

2. In the Menu, go to [Camera icon] → [DRIVE SETTING] → [BKT SETTING] → [BKT SELECT] → [ISO BKT].

3. Within [BKT SETTING], choose [ISO BKT].

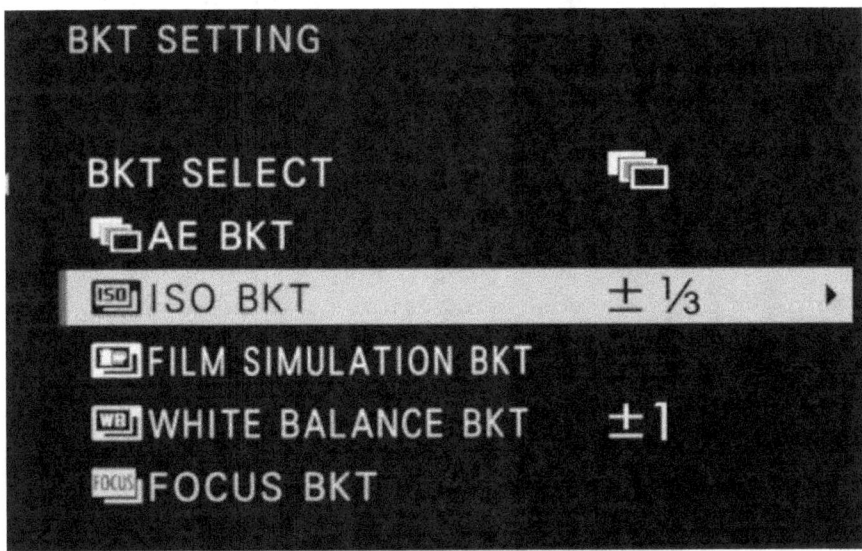

4.  Pick a bracket amount: [+-1/3], [+-2/3], or [+-1].

5.  Press the shutter button to capture 3 images with different ISO settings.

### *White Balance BKT*

When you use WHITE BALANCE BKT on your camera, it works like this: when you snap a picture, the camera first captures it with the white balance setting you have at that moment. But here's the cool part - it doesn't stop there! It also makes two more versions of the same picture. One is a bit adjusted to have slightly more fine-tuning, and the other is adjusted to have slightly less fine-tuning.

### Using White Balance Bracketing

1.  Turn the dial to <BKT>.

2.  Go to <MENU> and follow this path: [Camera icon] → [DRIVE SETTING] → [BKT SETTING] → [BKT SELECT] → [WHITE BALANCE BKT].

3.  In the [BKT SETTING] menu, choose [WHITE BALANCE BKT].

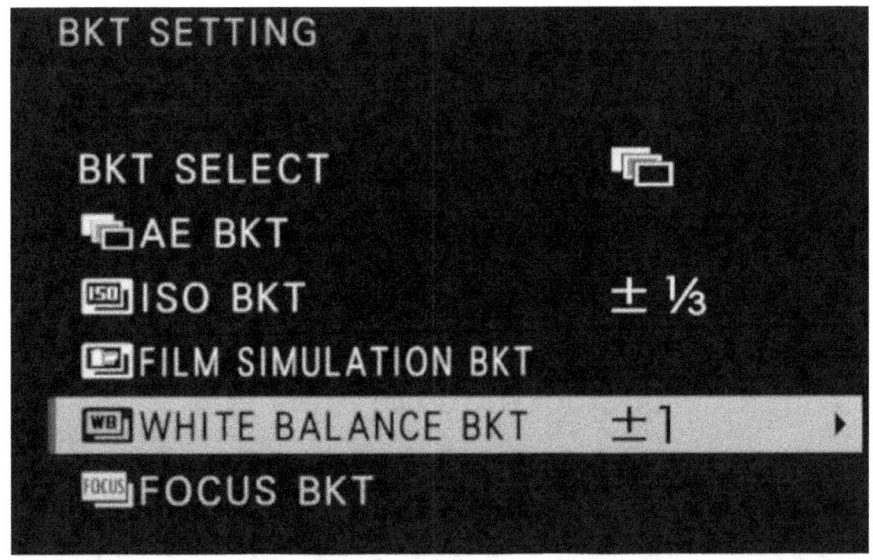

4. Pick the bracket amount: [+/-1], [+/-2], or [+/-3].

5. Press the shutter button to capture 3 images with different white balance settings.

### *Auto Exposure Bracket*

With AE BKT, your camera takes a picture with the current exposure setting. After that, it automatically creates extra copies of the image based on the number of shots you choose. This results in pictures with increased and decreased exposure as per your selection.

Auto Exposure Bracket recording helps you take better photos with more details. It works by taking multiple shots with different exposures. One shot captures bright areas well, while another captures dark areas. Later, you can combine these shots to get an overall photo with details in both bright and dark parts. To use AE bracket, set the difference in exposure, the order of shots, and how many shots you want to take.

## Configuring AE Bracket Settings

1. Turn the dial to <BKT> on your camera.

2. In the Menu, go to [DRIVE SETTING] → [BKT SETTING] → [BKT SELECT] → [AE BKT].

3. Back in [BKT SETTING], choose [AE BKT].

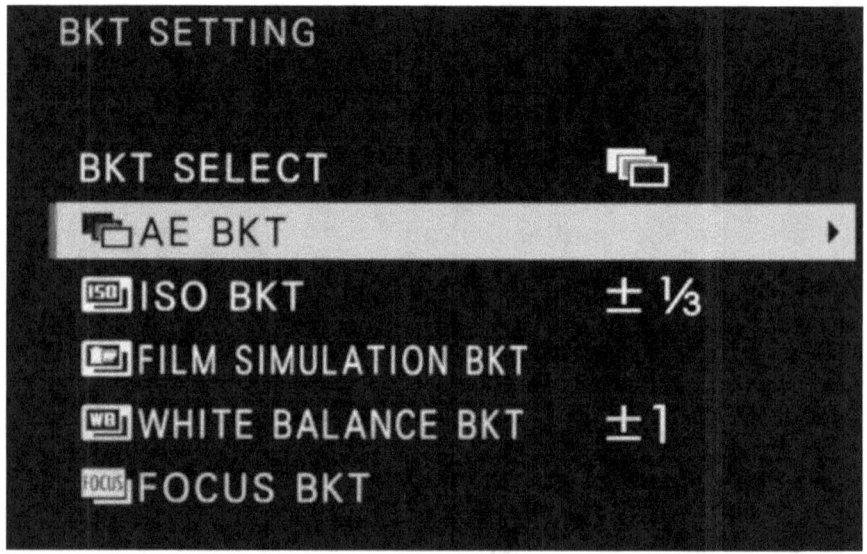

4. Set the following options:

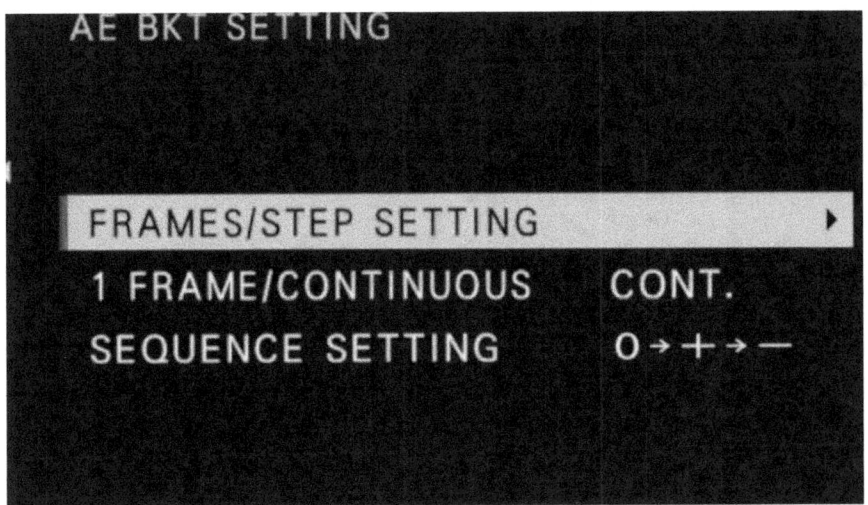

- [FRAMES]: Decide how many shots you want for AE Bracket shooting.

- [STEP]: Choose how much exposure should vary between each shot.

- [1 FRAME/CONTINUOUS]: Decide if shots are taken one at a time or continuously when you press and hold the shutter button.

- [SEQUENCE SETTING]: Choose the order of bracketed shots, like normal exposure followed by overexposure and then underexposure.

After you set up the AE bracketing, push the shutter button to start taking a series of photos with different exposures.

### *Film Simulation Bracket*

With FILM SIMULATION BKT, your camera can capture a photo using three different film styles you choose. If you're unsure which style suits your image, take multiple shots with various film simulations. Later, pick the one you like the most by setting your preferred film simulation types for the bracket recording.

### Configuring Film Simulation Bracket Settings

1. Turn the dial to <BKT>.

2. In the Menu, go to [Camera icon] > [DRIVE SETTING] > [BKT SETTING] > [BKT SELECT] > [FILM SIMULATION BKT].

3. On the [BKT SETTING] menu, choose [FILM SIMULATION BKT].

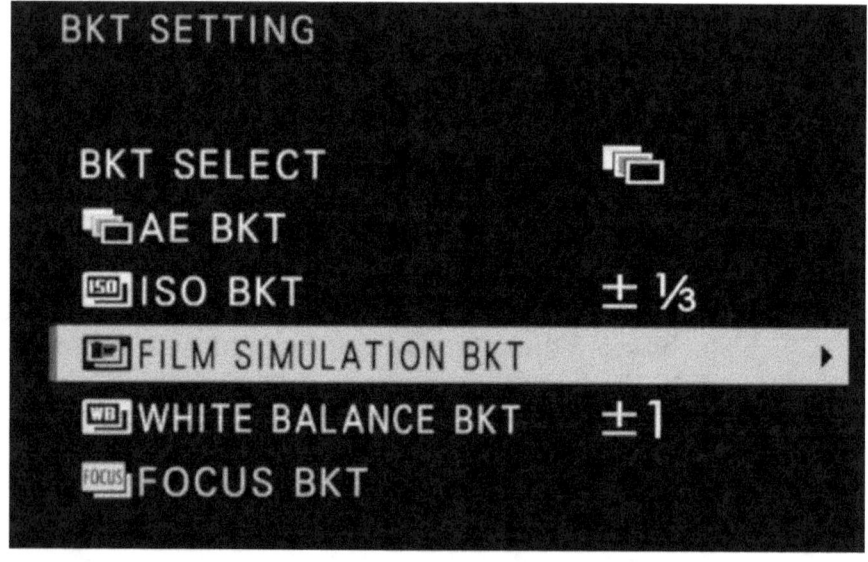

4. Pick [FILM 1], [FILM 2], or [FILM 3].

5. Choose a film simulation.

After choosing the film simulations for the bracket, start recording by pressing the shutter button.

# HDR

Cameras have limits in capturing both bright and dark parts of a scene. Have you ever noticed when you take a photo against a bright window, either the outside is well-lit, but the person is dark, or the person is fine, but the bright background is overexposed? If there's too much contrast, the camera might struggle to capture both well. High Dynamic Range (HDR) helps the camera balance this contrast for a better photo.

HDR, or High Dynamic Range, takes several pictures at different exposures. The camera snaps one for what it thinks is the right exposure, another for dark areas, and another for bright areas. Then combine these pictures to make one image that shows details in both light and dark parts.

To get a clear picture, keep the camera still when taking multiple shots. The final image might be a bit smaller because the resolution can drop.

### *Shooting HDR*

1. Turn the dial to <HDR>.

2. Navigate to <MENU> → [Camera icon] → [DRIVE SETTING] → [HDR MODE].

3. Choose from these options:

- **[AUTO]:** Camera picks HDR from 200% to 800%

- **[200%]:** Set dynamic range to 200%

- **[400%]:** Set dynamic range to 400%

- **[800%]:** Set dynamic range to 800%

- **[800%+]:** Maximum dynamic range variation.

4.  Press the shutter to take multiple photos that merge into a single image.

## Paranormas

If your camera's widest view isn't enough to capture the entire scene in just one photo, you have an option! Instead of settling for a partial shot, you can take several pictures from different viewpoints and then merge them into one huge image. This combined image is called a panorama. The X-T5 makes it easy for you with its Panorama mode, automatically piecing together these photos to create a single, wide-ranging panorama photo.

### *Taking a Panorama Photo*

1.  Turn the dial to "Panorama."

2.  Use the left/right buttons to pick how wide you want your panorama, then press the "MENU/OK" button.

3.  Pick the direction for your panorama using the left/right buttons, then press "MENU/OK."

4. Stand still, face the middle of where your photo will be, and turn your body to capture the whole scene. Or use a tripod. Press the shutter button, rotate toward the arrow on the screen, and let go. The camera stops automatically when it finishes capturing the scene.

**Tip:** Have a friend take a wide photo of you from left to right. Stand still first, then quickly move behind your friend and strike different poses. This way, you'll have a cool panorama of yourself in various positions.

## Multiple Exposures

The Fujifilm X-T5 has a neat trick that can make your flower pictures look really special. Here's how it works: you can take up to 9 pictures of the same flower but in different places around it. Then, using a special option in the Menu (not on the drive dial), you can blend all those pictures into one. It's like having a magic power to make it seem as if there are lots of flowers in the final photo, even though you only took a picture of one! It's a bit like arranging your favorite toys in different positions and then magically combining them into a fantastic group photo..

### *Taking a Multiple Exposure Photograph*

1. Go to the camera settings by selecting <MENU>, then choose the [Camera icon], followed by [MULTI EXPOSURE], and turn it [ON].

2. Choose a mode:

- **[ADDITIVE]:** Combine exposures; adjust exposure compensation based on the number of shots.

- **[AVERAGE]:** Camera adjusts exposure for a well-exposed final image.

- **[BRIGHT]:** Select the brightest pixel at each location, potentially mixing colors.

- **[DARK]:** Selects the darkest pixel at each location, potentially mixing colors.

3. Take the first picture.

4. After taking the first shot (e.g., a flower), press <MENU/OK>. The initial shot appears, and you can retake it with the < ◄ > button.

5. Take another shot.

6. Press <MENU/OK>. The first two images will be displayed together.

7. Repeat the process for up to 9 exposures. To retake the prior shot, use the < ◄ > button. Press <DISP/BACK> to finish the multiple-exposure image.

## Pixel Shift Multi Shot Pixel Shift

When you want to capture really clear and detailed still pictures with the Fujifilm X-T5, you can try out something called Multi-Shot. Here's how it works: the camera takes 20 pictures, each one with a tiny, gentle movement of the camera sensor. It's like taking lots of puzzle pieces that are slightly different and putting them together to create a super-detailed picture.

After you've taken these shots, you can use another tool called FUJIFILM Pixel Shift Combiner. This clever tool helps you blend all those 20 shots into one final picture that's super high-resolution and packed with details. It's like turning those puzzle pieces into a beautiful, clear picture that captures every little detail. So, if you want your photos to be super sharp and detailed, Multi-Shot and Pixel Shift Combiner are like a dynamic duo to make it happen!

### *Shooting with Pixel Shift Multi Shot*

1. Open the Menu, click the camera icon, and choose "PIXEL SHIFT MULTI SHOT."

2. Pick "INTERVAL" and set a value. Shorter values are suggested, but longer ones might be needed with a flash to let it recharge.

3. Press the shutter button to capture a series of images.

4. Use the FUJIFILM Pixel Shift Combiner software on a computer to merge the RAW images.

## Setting Resolution and File Type

### Image Quality

The Fujifilm X-T5 takes great pictures, especially considering its 40-megapixel camera. It produces clear photos with little to no noise at ISO 64 to 3200, although there's a bit more noise at

ISO 6400 and even more at ISO 12800 and 25600 (avoid ISO 51200).

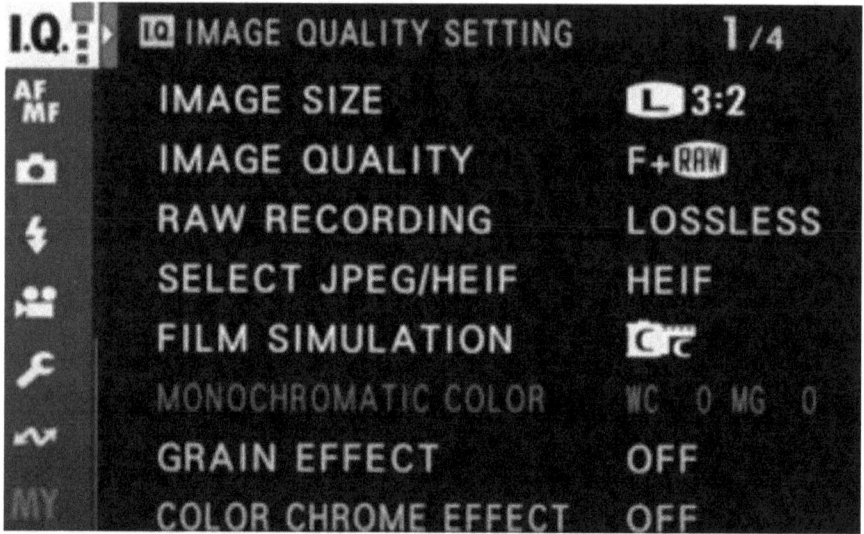

The RAW files also look good, though they may have more noise than the JPEGs. Night shots are fantastic, and the Bulb mode allows for longer exposures if needed, up to a maximum of 30 seconds, which is enough for most low-light photos. The camera has cool Film Simulation modes that give a vintage vibe, and features like Dynamic Range, HDR settings, and Advanced Filters help improve details in shadows and highlights, making it fun to experiment with your photos.

**Night**

If you enjoy snapping photos when it's dark outside, the Fujifilm X-T5 camera has a cool feature that lets you take pictures for a longer time. With the Time shutter speed option, you can capture images for as long as 30 seconds. And if you switch to Bulb mode, you can go even longer, taking pictures that last up to a whole hour, which is like having the camera open its eyes to gather light for a really long time to make sure your night photos look amazing. It's like having a magical tool that lets you capture the beauty of the night sky or city lights for as long as you want!

## Multi-Shot Pixel Shift

You can take super detailed 160-megapixel photos using a special Pixel Shift feature. The camera takes 20 shots in this process, moving the image sensor slightly in different directions each time. Afterward, you need to use the Pixel Shift Combiner software from Fujifilm's website to select and combine these 20 shots into one high-quality D.N.G. file.

## Multiple Exposure

The Fujifilm X-T5 camera has a cool trick – it can combine as many as nine pictures in different ways to create a new, special picture without needing any extra software. It's like putting together puzzle pieces to make a bigger picture! There are different modes you can choose, like additive, average, bright, or dark. Each mode gives your combined picture a unique look. So, if you want to blend a bunch of photos together and make something really cool, the X-T5 has got you covered. It's like having a creative tool right in your camera!

## Dynamic Range

The Fujifilm X-T5 has three dynamic range options: 100%, 200%, and 400%, with 100% being the default. You can also use Auto mode to let the camera decide. These settings affect how much detail you see in shadows and highlights, but using higher options may introduce more noise. Note that you can't completely turn off this function, which works up to ISO 500.

## HDR

The Fujifilm X-T5 camera comes with a special mode called High Dynamic Range (HDR), which can make your photos look extra amazing. There are five choices in this mode: AUTO, 200%, 400%, 800%, and 800%+. What happens is, when you pick one of these options, the camera takes three pictures super quickly, each with a different brightness level. Then, it cleverly combines these three photos to create one picture that looks awesome, with all the bright and dark parts perfectly balanced. It's like magic for your photos, making sure every detail looks just right!

## Film Simulators

The Fujifilm X-T5 camera is pretty cool because it gives you the power to make your photos look like they were taken with different kinds of old-fashioned films. It's like adding a special filter to your pictures. There are 19 options to choose from, each making your photos have a unique and nostalgic vibe. So, if you want your pictures to look like they were snapped with a classic film, the X-T5 has a bunch of settings for you to try out and have fun with!

## Advanced Filters

When you're about to take a picture with the Fujifilm X-T5 camera, it's like having a box of 13 special filters you can choose from to add a creative touch to your photo. You can see these filters right on the screen or through the viewfinder before you even click the picture button. It's a bit like trying on different pairs of glasses to see which one makes the world look the coolest before you take the shot. So, if you want to get creative with your photos, the X-T5 has a bunch of options for you to play around with and make your pictures extra special!

### *RAW vs. JPEG vs HEIF*

There are three types of compressed image files: RAW, JPEG, and HEIF. RAW files keep more image details but result in larger sizes. If you plan to edit photos, use RAW (like Fujifilm's .RAF). Keep in mind that not all software supports Fujifilm RAW. For easy playback on various devices, JPEG is more common, but it has less detailed information than RAW.

HEIF makes images look great and takes up less space than JPEG. It uses fancy tech to compress pictures. The downside is only some use it, so sharing and viewing options might be limited. If you want to check HEIF pics on a computer, remember to change the file extension from ".HIF" to ".HEIC." It usually happens automatically when you transfer pics from the camera to a computer with a USB cable.

### Setting the Image Compression Rate

1. Go to the Menu and find "IMAGE QUALITY" under "I.Q."

2.  Choose from the following options:

    - **[FINE]:** Saves high-quality JPEG or HEIF images with low compression.

    - **[NORMAL]:** Saves JPEG or HEIF images with higher compression for more storage but lower quality than [FINE].

    - **[FINE + RAW]:** Records both RAW and high-quality JPEG or HEIF images.

    - **[NORMAL + RAW]:** Records both RAW and normal-quality JPEG or HEIF images.

    - **[RAW]:** Records only a RAW file.

    To decide between JPEG and HEIF, follow these instructions.

## Select JPEG/HEIF

Choose between JPEG and HEIF formats in the Menu labeled "I.Q."

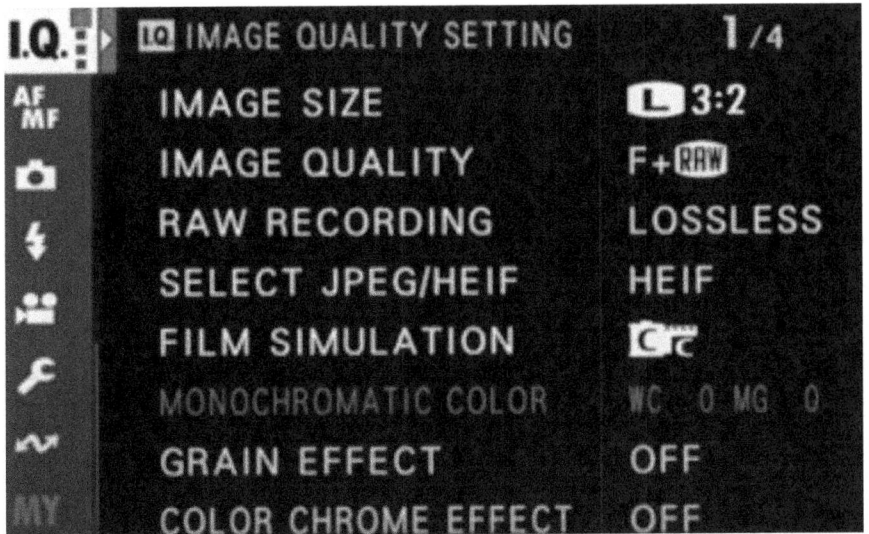

### RAW Image Toggle

To quickly decide whether you want to take high-quality RAW photos or regular ones, you can make it simple by linking the [RAW] choice to a button on your camera. Press this special button once, and your camera will switch to the settings on the right side of the table, allowing you to capture RAW photos with all their extra detail.

Press the button again, and it will go back to the regular settings on the left side of the table, so you can take regular photos without the extra fuss. It's like having a shortcut button to toggle between super-detailed and regular pictures.

| Currently selected option for [IMAGE QUALITY] | Behavior when [RAW] function button is pressed |
| --- | --- |
| FINE | FINE + RAW |
| NORMAL | NORMAL + RAW |
| FINE + RAW | FINE |
| NORMAL + RAW | NORMAL |
| RAW | FINE |

### *RAW Compression*

The X-T5 lets you choose how much to compress a RAW image.

### Setting the RAW Compression

1. Go to the menu, choose [I.Q], and select [RAW RECORDING].

2. When selecting, you have three options:

    - **[UNCOMPRESSED]:** Makes larger files without compressing the RAW images.

    - **[LOSSLESS COMPRESSED]:** Compresses RAW images with a reversible algorithm, keeping

70

good quality and allowing viewing with specific software.

- **[COMPRESSED]:** Uses a non-reversible compression algorithm, making files 25 to 35 percent smaller while maintaining quality similar to [UNCOMPRESSED].

# Image Size

### *Aspect Ratio*

The aspect ratio of a picture tells you how wide it is compared to how tall it is. It's like looking at a rectangle and figuring out if it's more wide or more tall. When you see numbers like 1920 x 1080 or 1280 x 720, they represent this ratio. For example, 1920 x 1080 has a ratio of 16:9, which means it's 16 units wide for every 9 units of height. Another example is 640 x 480, which has a 4:3 ratio.

If you're making a video for an older TV with a 4:3 ratio, like those old square-shaped ones, it's a good idea to set your camera's ratio to 4:3 as well. This way, when you watch your video on that TV, it fits nicely on the screen without looking stretched or squished. It's like making sure your puzzle piece matches the space it's supposed to go in.

### *Picture Size*

You have different choices when it comes to the size of your pictures. The number of tiny dots, called pixels, in your picture affects how detailed it looks. If you have more pixels, your picture will have more details, but it will also take up more space on your computer or phone. You can choose different sizes depending on the shape of your picture. Here are some options:

## Sizes available for a [3:2] aspect ratio

| Setting | Image Size |
|---|---|
| [L] | 7728 x 5152 pixels |
| [M] | 5472 x 3648 pixels |
| [S] | 3888 x 2592 pixels |
| [M] SPORTS FINDER MODE with 1.25X CROP | 6000 x 4000 pixels |

## Sizes available for a [16:9] aspect ratio

| Setting | Image Size |
|---|---|
| [L] | 7728 x 4244 pixels |
| [M] | 5472 x 3080 pixels |

| [S] | 3888 x 2184 pixels |
|---|---|
| [M] SPORTS FINDER MODE with 1.25X CROP | 6000 x 3376 pixels |

## Sizes available for a [1:1] aspect ratio

| Setting | Image Size |
|---|---|
| [L] | 5152 x 5152 pixels |
| [M] | 3648 x 3648 pixels |
| [S] | 2592 x 2592 pixels |
| [M] SPORTS FINDER MODE with 1.25X CROP | 4000 x 4000 pixels |

## Sizes available for a [4:3] aspect ratio

| Setting | Image Size |
|---|---|
| [L] | 5664 x 5152 pixels |
| [M] | 4864 x 3648 pixels |
| [S] | 2456 x 2592 pixels |
| [M] SPORTS FINDER MODE with 1.25X CROP | 5328 x 4000 pixels |

## Sizes available for a [5:4] aspect ratio

| Setting | Image Size |
|---|---|
| [L] | 6432 x 5152 pixels |
| [M] | 4560 x 3648 pixels |
| [S] | 3264 x 2592 pixels |
| [M] SPORTS FINDER MODE with 1.25X CROP | 4992 x 4000 pixels |

# CHAPTER 4: TAKING CHARGE OF EXPOSURE

## Introducing the Exposure Trio: Aperture, Shutter Speed, and ISO

To capture good pictures, controlling how much light enters your camera is essential. Light comes in through the lens and can be controlled by the lens opening (aperture) and the shutter. It helps in creating better-quality images.

Exposure is like how much light the camera gets. Think of it like Goldilocks – not too much light (overexposure), not too little (underexposure), but just right.

There's this trio called the exposure triangle – aperture, shutter speed, and ISO. Picture it as a stable triangle for the right exposure. If you mess with one part (like changing the aperture), the others (shutter speed, ISO) need adjusting to keep things balanced.

### Aperture

Think of the aperture as the camera's special eye. Now, this eye can change its size, and we measure that using something called an F-number. The F-number is like a secret code that tells us how big or small the eye is.

When the F-number is low, like f/1, it means the eye is wide open, like when you're super excited. But when the F-number is high, like f/16, it means the eye is a bit squinted, like when you're looking at something tiny.

Now, here's the cool part: when the eye is wide open (low F-number), it lets in a lot of light really fast. This is like turning on a super bright flashlight for the camera, and it helps take pictures quickly. So, if you want to capture moments in a snap, you'd go for a big opening (small F-number). It's like giving your camera the power to see things in a flash!

### *Aperture and Light*

Think of the camera lens like the eye of a curious explorer. The bigger the eye, the more light it can gather. So, when it's a bit dim or dark, you want to make that camera eye bigger by adjusting its hole (called the aperture). Now, instead of using complicated numbers, we keep it simple: a lower number means a bigger hole.

So, here's the trick: if your surroundings are not so bright, tell the camera to make its eye bigger by choosing a lower number (they call it the f-number). This lets in more light, making your picture brighter and clearer, just like turning on a little flashlight for your camera. It's like giving your camera the power to see better in the dark!

## Sunny 16 Rule

When you're out on a bright and sunny day, there's a handy trick called the "Sunny 16 Rule" that can make your photos look just right. What you do is set your camera's aperture to a special number called f/16. It's like a secret code that helps your camera capture the perfect amount of sunlight, making sure your photo isn't too bright or too dark. So, when the sun is shining, remember the number 16, and your pictures will come out looking fantastic!

## Looney 11 Rule

When you're all set to take pictures of the moon in the night sky, there's a cool trick called the "Looney 11 Rule" that can make things easier. What you do is set your camera's aperture to a special number called f/11. It's like a little moon magic that helps your camera capture the moon's beauty just right, without making it too bright or too dim. So, if you're out there with your camera and the moon is shining, remember the number 11, and you'll capture those moonlit moments like a pro!

### *Aperture and Depth of Field*

The size of the opening in the camera, the aperture, is crucial because it influences how much of the picture is sharp. A big aperture makes a smaller area in focus, so the subject is sharp, and the surroundings are blurry. A small aperture includes more of the background in focus. Remember, a higher f-number means more focus, while a lower f-number means less focus.

### *Aperture and Bokeh*

When you snap a picture and the background looks all fuzzy and dreamy, that's what experts call a "shallow depth of field."

Now, here's a fun bonus: when the lights in the blurry part look like beautiful blobs of softness, that's called "bokeh." Bokeh is a fancy word from Japan that's all about that lovely, out-of-focus effect.

The cool part? Your camera lens and how wide or narrow the opening is (that's the aperture) can give you different shapes of bokeh. It's like having a bunch of magical tools. Some lenses make bokeh that looks like perfect circles, while others create bokeh with unique shapes like triangles or squares.

### *Aperture and Sun Stars*

Have you ever noticed those cool pictures or videos where the sun looks like a shiny star with rays of light shooting out? Well, you can create that magical effect yourself! All you have to do is tinker with your camera settings by making the opening a bit smaller. It's like adjusting a magical door to capture those beautiful sunbeams.

The more blades your camera lens has, the more rays you'll be able to capture, making it even more dazzling. But, and this is important, never stare directly at the sun, and avoid keeping your camera pointed at it for too long. Doing so could be harmful and might damage your camera. So, create those starry sunbursts, but always be kind to your eyes and your camera!

## Shutter speed

In photography, shutter speed is how long the camera shutter stays open. It's also called exposure time because it's about how much light reaches the film or sensor. In videos, shutter speed is how long each frame is exposed, usually ranging from a few seconds to a fraction of a second.

### *How Does Shutter Speed Affect the Look of My Footage?*

Photography

When you take pictures, the speed at which your camera's shutter opens and closes makes a big difference. If you use a slow shutter speed, things that are moving might appear blurry in your photos. On the other hand, if you go for a fast shutter speed, you can freeze the action and capture fast-moving things really clearly.

Think about photos of ocean waves that look all smooth and dreamy. That's likely because the photographer chose a slow shutter speed. This makes the moving water blend together, giving it that silky, flowing appearance. So, in photography, the speed of your shutter helps you decide whether things in your pictures will look sharp and crisp or all soft and flowing.

Videography

Slowing down the shutter in videos makes things look blurrier and smoother while speeding it up makes images sharper, but motion might seem jittery. It applies when capturing moving objects or when you're moving the camera.

When shooting videos, a simple guideline is to set your shutter speed close to double your frame rate. For example, if you're filming at 24 frames per second, aim for a shutter speed of around 1/48. This is called the rule of using a 180-degree shutter. However, adjust the shutter speed to achieve different visual effects. Keep it consistent across your entire video project unless you have a specific reason to change it.

If you're recording video under fluorescent lights and see flickering or filming a screen with scan lines, changing the shutter speed can help lessen the flicker or scan lines. For photos, you can use the camera's flicker reduction feature to sync the shutter with the lights and reduce flickering.

### Configuring Flicker Reduction

1. Go to the menu, click the camera icon, and select "Flicker Reduction."

2. Choose one of the following options:

   - **All Frames:** Reduces flicker in all images taken in a rapid series, but it might slow the shooting speed.

   - **First Frame:** Measures flicker only before the first image in a series and applies the same reduction to all following frames.

   - **Off:** No flicker reduction is applied.

### Flickerless S.S Setting

The Flickerless S.S Setting is like a more advanced way to reduce flickering, and you can use it when you're in Shutter Priority <S> or Manual <M> mode on your camera. It's super handy when you're dealing with flickers that happen really fast, especially those coming from LED lights, not the usual fluorescent ones.

When you switch on the Flickerless S.S Setting, you get to make tiny adjustments to how quickly your camera's shutter opens and closes. This helps your camera sync up with the flickering of a light source, like a TV or computer screen. If your camera's rhythm doesn't match the screen's rhythm, you might see some flickering or weird stripes moving on the screen. So, turning on the Flickerless S.S Setting is like a cool trick to avoid those distracting flickers and make your photos look even better.

## ISO

Think of ISO as a special setting in your camera that decides how sensitive it is to light. When you set a low ISO, like 100, it's great for sunny days because your camera becomes less sensitive to light. On the other hand, when it's dark, a higher ISO is helpful to make your camera more light-sensitive.

However, if you set the ISO too high, your pictures might end up looking grainy and not so clear. So, it's usually a good idea to keep the ISO low for nice and clear pictures. Before you take important shots, it's a smart move to test your camera to figure out the best ISO levels for the lighting conditions.

# CHAPTER 5: CAPTURING VIDEO

## Recording Movies

To make a video, switch the mode dial to "MOVIE." Then, you can use different recording modes like Program AE, Aperture-Priority AE, Shutter-Priority AE, and Manual Exposure. Press the shutter button to start recording. You'll see a recording indicator and the remaining recording time on the display. A red border means regular recording and a green border indicates high-speed recording. The display shows the time left and the elapsed time while recording. Press the shutter button again to stop recording.

## REC Frame Indicator

Normally, when your camera is recording, it shows a red frame on the screen to tell you that it's capturing video. This red frame is like a little signal that lets you know the camera is actively recording. However, if you prefer, you have the option to turn off this red frame indicator. This means you can decide whether or not you want the camera to visibly show that it's recording by either keeping or turning off the red frame.

### Turning the Recording Frame Indicator on/off

Choose "Movie Mode" from the menu, then select whether you want to turn the "REC Frame Indicator" on or off.

# Video Resolution

Video resolution is the size of a movie. It's not about how big the file is in megabytes or gigabytes, but rather the dimensions of the movie frame in pixels. The usual sizes are 4K (3840 x 2160), Full HD (1920 x 1080), HD (1280 x 720), and Standard Definition (640 x 480). If you want the best quality on big HD or 4K TVs, go for 4K or Full HD.

If you need more clarification about the video size, choose 4K for the best quality. You can make it smaller later without losing quality. If you start with a smaller size, enlarging it later reduces picture quality. Use standard definition for less memory space or faster internet downloads.

What do the resolution numbers mean? Well, resolution is how many tiny dots (pixels) form a TV or monitor screen. Each dot shows a color to create the whole picture. More pixels mean a clearer picture. In numbers like 1920 x 1080, the first is width, the second is height. So, 1920 x 1080 means 1920 dots across and 1080 dots up and down, making 2,073,600 pixels.

# Frame Rate

Think of a video as a collection of pictures that play in a fast sequence, like a flipbook. The frame rate, also known as FPS (frames per second), tells us how many pictures are taken every second to make the video. If the frame rate is higher, it means more pictures are captured in each second, making the video smoother and more detailed. So, when we say "higher frame rate," we mean more pictures per second, and that makes the video look better.

## Which Frame Rate to Choose?

Movies look best at 24 frames per second because they give a natural feel and are suitable for the web. Depending on the region, TV shows are usually shot at 30 fps for a more realistic look. If you're making content for TV, it's recommended to use the frame rate that matches the broadcasting standard in your region—30 fps for NTSC (used in most of the Americas) and 25 fps for PAL (used in Europe and parts of Asia).

Filmmakers use 60 fps or higher for cool effects like slow motion. They shoot faster than needed and then slow the footage to 24 fps. At 60 fps, moving things look sharper and more vivid, creating a hyper-real feeling. This frame rate is excellent for sports or action shots. The blur in your footage also depends on your shutter speed settings and the frame rate.

## Movie Mode

Now that we've discussed the video resolution and frame rate let's see what choices the X-T5 offers.

### Setting the Video Quality and Frame Rate

1. Open the menu and go to "Movie Mode."

2. Use the up and down buttons to choose a frame size and resolution.

3. Press the right arrow button and then use the up and down buttons to pick the frame rate.

# Movie File Format and Compression

The Fujifilm X-T5 lets you pick from 7 different types of movie files and how much they get compressed.

### H.264 vs H.265

The first part of how movies are saved and made smaller is codecs. A codec is like a computer trick that squishes video files so they don't take up too much space. There are two choices in the X-T5 camera: H.264 and H.265. H.264 is older but works with more things. H.265 is newer and makes files even smaller, but it's not as easy to work with, and some things might still need to be fully supported.

### All-I vs LongGOP

Now, let's talk about how the XT-5 compresses videos. There are two types: ALL-Intra (ALL-I) and Long GOP. Long GOP, or Long Group of Pictures, focuses on the changes in each frame. For instance, in a static interview background, where only the person being interviewed moves, Long GOP would be chosen to make a smaller video file.

All-Intra compression is a way of making videos where each frame is treated as essential and compressed individually. This method results in higher video quality and allows you to edit each frame separately. However, because it keeps much data, the video files become larger. It's best for videos with many changes between frames, like when you move the camera or record fast-paced action.

## 420 vs 422

The 3-digit number is like a code for colors in videos. Y is for brightness, U is for blue, and V is for red. It's called YUV, and it mixes brightness and color mathematically to make the final colors in a picture. There are two choices, 4:2:2 and 4:2:0. 4:2:2 is more accurate, capturing more colors, but it needs more computer power and makes bigger files. For most cases, 4:2:0 is good enough, especially if you need more editing later.

The end part of a movie file involves something called a container. A movie file isn't just the video; it includes sound, extra info, and more. All this stuff needs to be stored together, which we call a container. MOV and MP4 are two types of containers.

MOV works best with Apple devices, like iPhones or Macs. On the other hand, MP4 is more flexible and works well on many devices and apps. If you're making videos for social media, MP4 is great because it keeps good quality, has small file sizes, and is widely supported. But if you're all about top-notch image quality, MOV might be your pick, especially if you're using Apple gear.

## Bit Depth

Bit depth, or color depth, affects video quality by determining how many colors a camera can capture. More colors mean better video quality. For instance, 8-bit cameras can record over 16.7 million colors, while 10-bit cameras can capture over a billion colors due to their ability to record more color levels.

Most devices like TVs, computers, and smartphones show videos in 8-bit. Using 8-bit for recording is okay. However, using 10-bit gives you better control and quality when editing videos later. More colors in 10-bit means you can adjust brightness, contrast, and color more intensely without losing much quality. In 8-bit videos, editing the sky might cause solid strips of color, but 10-bit videos have more color information, making it less likely to have those color issues—similar to editing JPEG and RAW photos, where RAW has more info for better editing.

## Setting the Movie File Type and Compression

1. Choose your video recording settings by navigating through the menu: [Movie Mode] → [MEDIA REC SETTING] → [File Type and Compression].

2. Select of of your options:

   - **[H.264 ALL-I 420 MOV]:** High compression, 8-bit depth, All-I interframe compression, and 4:2:0 chroma sub-sampling.

   - **[H.264 LongGOP 420 MOV]:** High compression, 8-bit depth, Long GOP interframe compression, and 4:2:0 chroma sub-sampling.

   - **[H.264 LongGOP 420 MP4]:** Suitable for videos to be uploaded online.

- **[H.265 ALL-I 420 MOV]:** Higher compression, 10-bit depth, All-I interframe compression, and 4:2:0 chroma sub-sampling.

- **[H.265 LongGOP 420 MOV]:** Higher compression, 10-bit depth, Long GOP interframe compression, and 4:2:0 chroma sub-sampling.

- **[H.265 ALL-I 422 MOV]:** Higher compression, 10-bit depth, All-I interframe compression, and 4:2:2 chroma sub-sampling.

- **[H.265 LongGOP 422 MOV]:** Higher compression, 10-bit depth, Long GOP interframe compression, and 4:2:2 chroma sub-sampling.

## Data Level Setting

A video signal has both color and black-and-white information. Fujifilm gives you two options for the black-and-white part: [VIDEO RANGE] and [FULL RANGE]. With [VIDEO RANGE], 8-bit movies have black-and-white levels from 16 to 235, and 10-bit movies have levels from 64 to 940. With [FULL RANGE], 8-bit movies have levels from 0 to 255, and 10-bit movies have levels from 0 to 1023.

TVs see black as 16 and white as 235, while computers see black as 0 and white as 255. If you play a video meant for a TV on a computer, the colors might get messed up – blacks too dark and whites too bright. And if you play a TV video on a computer, the computer tries to make it work, but the quality might not be as good as a computer video.

If you're uploading a video without editing its brightness, contrast, or color, use 16-235 (VIDEO RANGE). If you'll edit and grade the footage, choose 0-255 (FULL RANGE) for more information and smoother tones in post-production.

### Setting the Luminance/ Data Level

1. Go to the menu, choose "Movie Mode," then select "Data Level Setting."

2. Pick a data level:

   - For "Video Range," the 8-bit signal range is 16-235, and the 10-bit signal range is 64-940.

   - For "Full Range," the 8-bit signal range is 0-255, and the 10-bit signal range is 0-1023.

## Movie Audio Settings

### Audio Level Display

When making a video, check your Microphone's audio levels to ensure you capture sound correctly. To turn on/off the audio level display, go to <MENU> → [Microphone] → [SCREEN SETTING] → [DISP. CUSTOM SETTING] and check [MIC LEVEL].

The audio level display shows soft at the bottom and loud at the top. If the display has no bars, there's no sound. Red bars at the top mean the sound is too loud for good recording. Aim for middle levels on the display for ideal audio.

## Audio Rec Level Adjustment

Adjusting the recording volume is like changing the sound level in your videos. If the sound is too quiet, you can make it louder by turning up the microphone level. On the other hand, if it's too loud and overwhelming, you can make it softer by turning the microphone level down. It's a bit like adjusting the volume on your TV or radio – you want it to be just right so that the sound in your videos sounds good and not too soft or too loud. So, if things are not sounding the way you want, just tweak the microphone level until it's just perfect for your ears.

### Setting the Audio Rec Level for the Internal Microphone

1. Go to the menu, select "Microphone," and then choose "Internal Mic Level Adjustment."

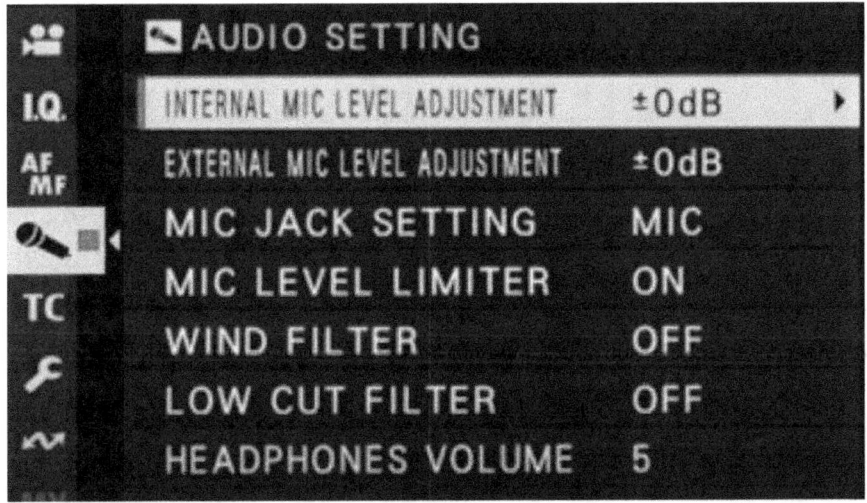

2. Choose one of the following options:

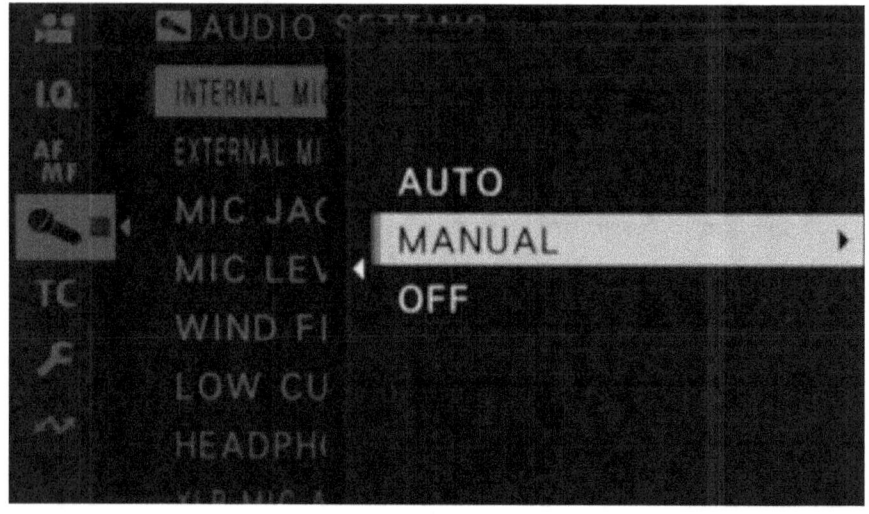

- **[AUTO]:** Let the camera automatically set the internal microphone sound level.

- **[MANUAL]:** Adjust the microphone level manually by tilting the focus stick to the right, choosing from 25 recording levels.

- **[OFF]:** Turn off the built-in Microphone.

You can also use an external microphone by plugging it into the camera's 3.5mm jack. Note that microphones requiring plug-in power won't work. If you use an external microphone, you can adjust audio input levels, but you'll need to do it in a different menu.

**Setting the Audio Rec Level for an External Microphone**

1. Go to the menu, choose [Microphone], and select [EXTERNAL MIC LEVEL ADJUSTMENT].

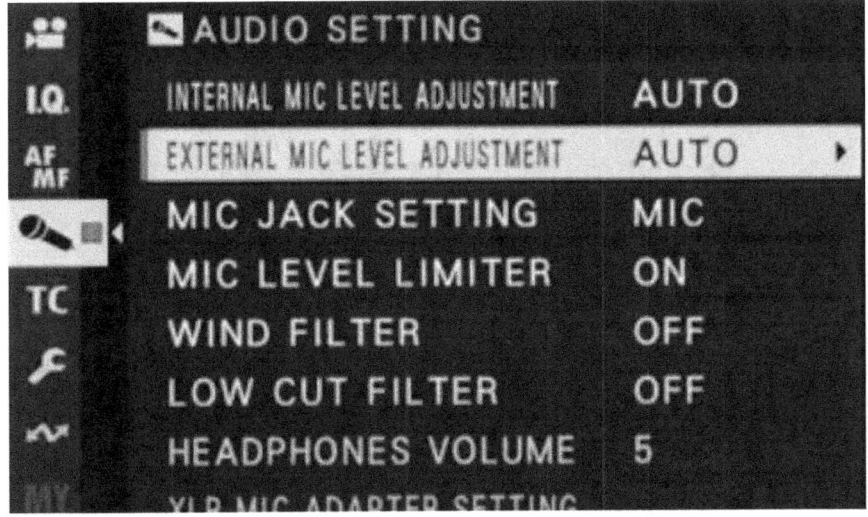

2. Choose:

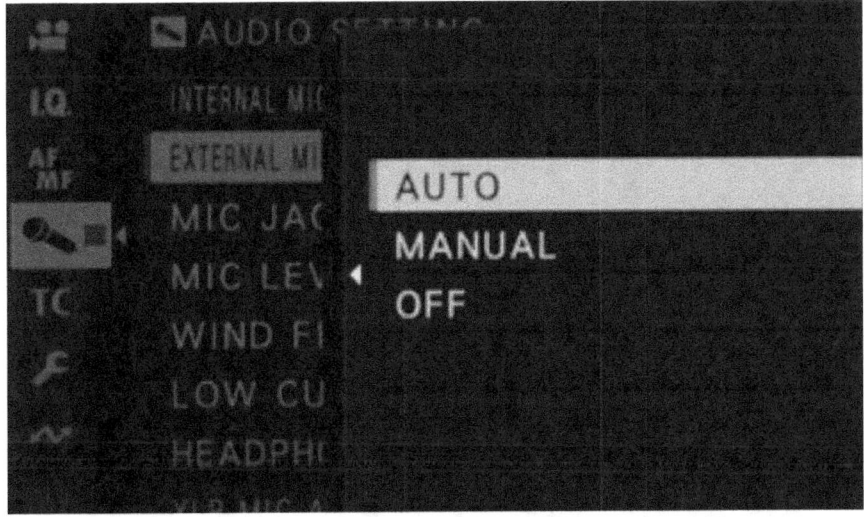

- **[AUTO]:** Let the camera set your external microphone sound level.

93

- **[MANUAL]:** Adjust the microphone level yourself using the focus stick. Tilt it right to pick from 25 recording levels.

- **[OFF]:** Stop the external Microphone from recording sound.

## Microphone Level Limiter

When you're getting ready to record, it's important to think about how loud the audio is going to be. You can control this by turning a knob or pressing some buttons to make the sound softer or louder. Now, here's a nifty feature to keep in mind: it's called the Mic Level Limiter. Think of it like a superhero for your audio – it jumps in to save the day and prevents the sound from getting all messy and distorted when it's too loud for the microphone.

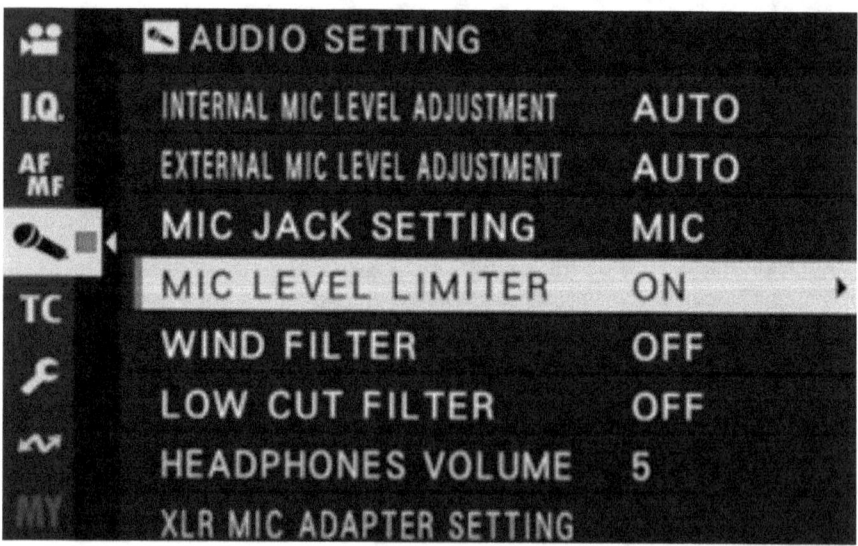

## Turning the Microphone Level Limiter on/off

Select the microphone option in the menu, then choose whether to turn the mic level limiter on or off.

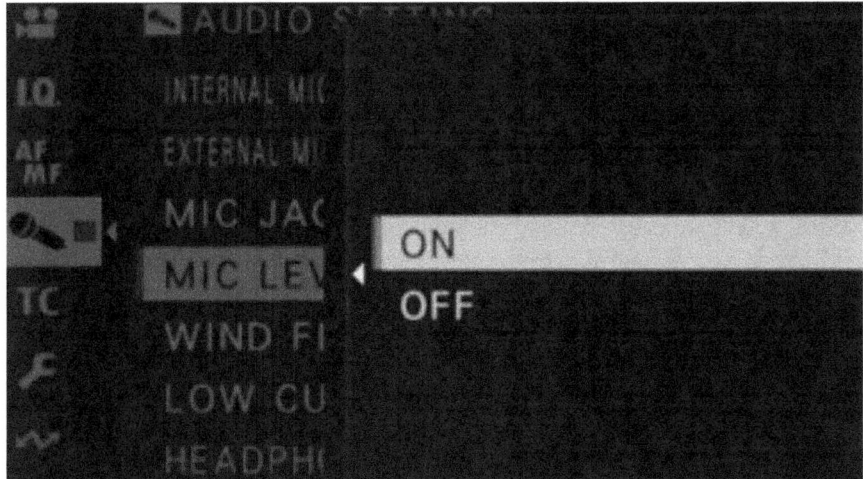

## Wind Noise Reduction

When you're recording videos in a windy spot, the wind can make a loud noise in your camera's microphone. This noise might distract from or cover up the sounds you actually want to capture. But don't worry, there's a solution! Your camera comes with something called a Wind Filter built right in.

You can turn this on, and it helps to lessen the windy noise, making your video sound much better and getting rid of that pesky wind distraction. So, next time you're out in the breeze filming, just flip on the Wind Filter to keep your audio sounding nice and clear.

## Turning the Wind Filter on/off

Select the menu, then choose the microphone option. After that, decide whether to turn the wind filter on or off.

## Low Cut Filter

When you're making videos, think about switching on the low-cut filter for better sound quality. This filter does a cool job—it helps cut down on unwanted background noises, like the hum of a fridge or the sound of cars passing by. It works by reducing those low-frequency noises that might sneak into your audio and make it sound not-so-great. So, it's like giving your videos a cleaner and clearer sound by saying "no thanks" to the distracting hums and rumbles in the background.

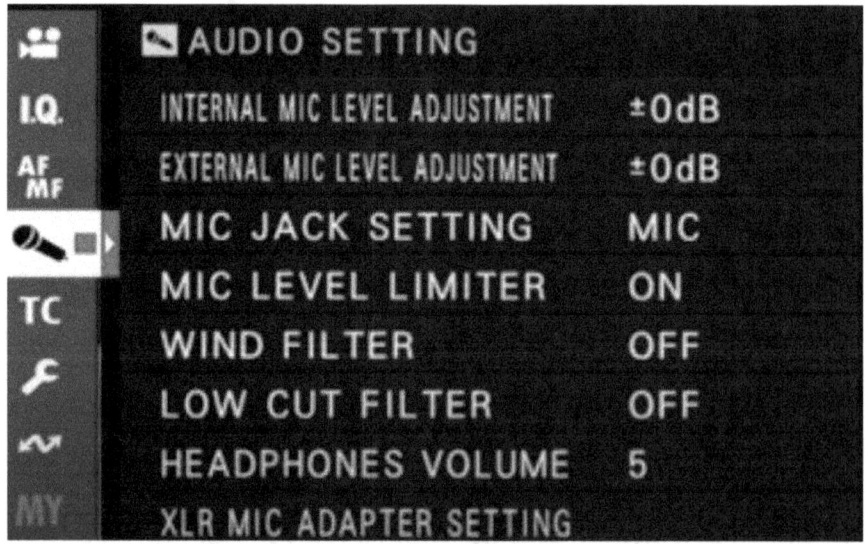

## Turning the Low Cut Filter on/off

Choose whether to turn the Low Cut Filter on or off in the menu by selecting the Microphone option.

## Headphone Volume

You can adjust the volume using the camera menu if your headphones are plugged into the camera.

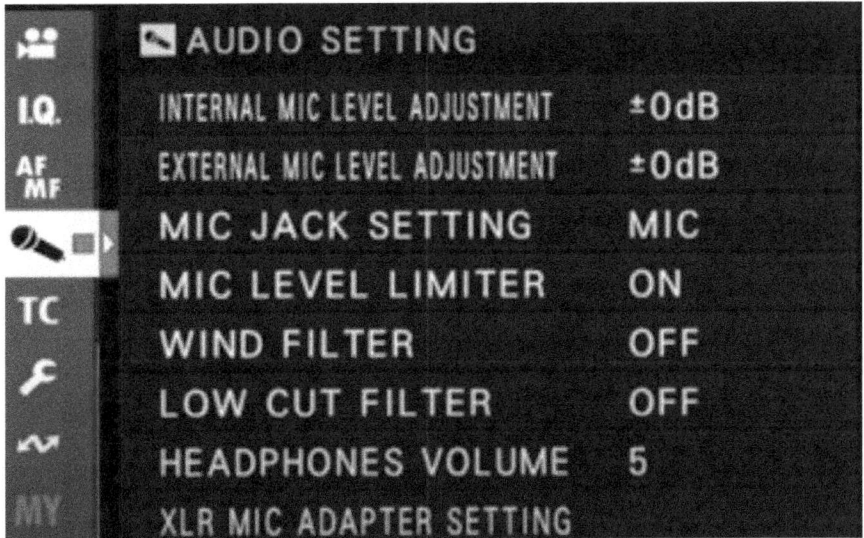

### Adjusting Headphone Volume

Choose "Microphone" from the menu, then adjust the volume for your headphones.

# Time Code Settings

Time code is like a special code that helps make sure videos from different cameras match up perfectly. When all the cameras use the same time code, it's much easier to sync, or line up, their videos when you're putting everything together during editing.

The usual time code standard is called "SMPTE Time Code," which stands for the Society of Motion Picture and Television Engineers. This time code follows a format that looks like this: HH (hours):MM (minutes):SS (seconds).oo (fractions of a second). So, it's like a language that cameras speak to each other, making sure they're all on the same page and capturing moments at the exact same time. This way, when you're editing, everything fits together seamlessly. It follows the format HH:MM:SS.oo.

### Turning the Time Code Display on/off

Go to the MENU, select TC, choose TIME CODE DISPLAY, and pick either ON or OFF.

## Start Time Setting

Setting the time code display can be done in three different ways to suit your needs. First, there's the option to choose [RESET], which makes the time code start from 00:00:00 – it's like resetting a clock to zero.

Another way is to start the time code from the current time, so it continues from where it is right now. Lastly, you can manually choose a specific starting time. This is similar to how cameras sync with external devices by entering a particular time in [MANUAL PRESET]. So, you have these three ways to decide how your time code begins, depending on what works best for you!

### Set the Time Code Start Time

1. Go to the menu, then choose "Start Time Setting."

2. Choose one of these options:

   - **Manual Input:** Move the focus stick to the right to set the time code yourself.

   - **Current Time:** Set the time code start time to the current time.

   - **Reset:** Reset the time code to 00:00:00:00.

## Count Up Setting

Choose how you want the time code to move forward.

### Configuring the Time Code Count Up Setting

1. Go to the menu, choose "TC," and select "COUNT UP SETTING."

2. Choose between:

   - **Rec Run:** Time code advances only when recording.

   - **Free Run:** Time code advances continuously, whether the camera is recording. It helps sync multiple cameras during live events, allowing you to match footage at specific time points across different cameras.

## Drop Frame

When you're shooting videos at certain speeds, like 59.94 frames per second or 29.97 frames per second, there are two ways to keep track of time: drop frame and non-drop frame. The timecode is based on 30 frames or 60 frames per second, even though the actual video speed is around 29.97 or 59.94 frames per second.

This difference can cause a gap between the timecode and the actual time during long recordings. Drop frame mode helps fix this gap by skipping a few frames, kind of like how we add a leap year every four years to account for the extra ¼ day in the calendar year. It's a way to make sure the timecode stays accurate even with these speed differences.

### *How to Set Whether to Drop Frames or Not*

1.  < MENU> → [TC] → [DROP FRAME]

2.  Choose from the options:

    - **[ON]:** If set to [ON], the camera drops frames to match the time code and recording time.

    - **[OFF]:** If set to [OFF], the time code is recorded without dropping frames.

You can also decide if the time code is shown on connected HDMI devices.

*Enable/Disable Time Codeon HDMI Output*

Go to MENU, then select TC, followed by HDMI TIME CODE OUTPUT, where you can choose ON or OFF.

# Tally Light Settings

When you're recording a video, the camera will have a light that turns on. This light is called the tally light. It can be at the back or the front of the camera, and you can decide if you want it to blink or stay on. This helps you know when the camera is actively recording.

## How to Set the Tally Light

1. Go to the menu, choose "Movie Mode," then select "TALLY LIGHT."

2. Choose from these options:

   - **[FRONT OFF REAR ]:** The rear indicator lamp stays on continuously while recording.

   - **[FRONT OFF REAR ]:** The rear indicator lamp blinks while recording.

   - **[FRONT REAR ]:** The front AF assists, and rear indicator lamps stay on continuously while recording.

   - **[FRONT REAR OFF]:** The front AF assist lamp stays on continuously, and the rear indicator lamp blinks while recording.

- **[FRONT  REAR ]:** The front AF assist lamp and rear indicator lamp blink while recording.

- **[FRONT REAR OFF]:** The front AF assist lamp blinks while recording.

- **[FRONT OFF REAR OFF]:** The front AF assist lamp and rear indicator lamp stay off during recording.

# CONCLUSION

You've reached the end of this book on the Fujifilm X-T5 User Guide. By now, you should have a deep understanding of this powerful camera's capabilities, from its intuitive controls and customizable settings to its advanced features and film simulations. You've explored shooting modes, mastered exposure and focus, and discovered the magic of creative options.

But this guide is just the beginning. Remember, the true depth of the X-T5 lies in your own artistic vision. Use your newfound knowledge to experiment, push boundaries, and capture the world in your unique way.

www.ingramcontent.com/pod-product-compliance
Lightning Source LLC
Chambersburg PA
CBHW071209290526
45796CB00008B/196